# The New Muslim's Field Guide

*Theresa Corbin & Kaighla Um Dayo*

*The New Muslim's Field Guide* / Theresa Corbin and Kaighla White. —1st ed.
ISBN-13: 978-1981328994
ISBN-10: 1981328998

# Contents

## Acknowledgments

Before anything, we must confess that all thanks and praise are without a doubt due to Allah (SWT). We bear witness that there is no god but God and that Prophet Muhammad (PBUH) is His final Messenger. We ask Allah to bless the new Muslims and allow this book to be a tool of guidance for them. This book could not have been possible without the help of many of our great friends, colleagues, and mentors. No woman (or man) is an island: we need each other to grow. We'd like to specifically thank Gracie Lawrence for her patience and guidance and Alta Sacra for her vital feedback on the cover design. We'd like to also thank Alta Sacra, too, as well as Candace Cooper for their incredibly valuable contributions in editing. Many thanks to our beta readers- James Campbell, Maryam C. Lautenschlager, and Kiran Awan. We'd also like to sincerely thank our husbands and families for their support and contribution to our project. Much thanks to all those who encouraged and pushed us to have the confidence to make this book a reality.

*"And He found you lost and guided [you ...]"*

*—Quran 93:7*

*Dedicated to all the converts who have struggled
to find their place in the ummah.*

# Introduction

I t's a chilly November morning. Mary is sitting in her car as the proverbial butterflies flutter about her stomach. Finally, her friend, Salwa, pulls up next to her and they hug briefly in the parking lot, and enter the domed building. Inside, she is not sure why, but she removes her shoes as her friend has done. She readjusts the fabric she haphazardly tossed over her hair and compares it to Salwa's skillfully-wrapped scarf.

Once they reach their destination inside, a mic opens, and Mary hears a smooth South-East Asian accent saying strange things in a foreign tongue. She's utterly lost, but assumes it's only a matter of time before they fall off her tongue just as easily. Finally, the voice from the mic says, "And now, we have a sister who has decided to make *shadada*[1] today, *mashaAllah tabarakAllah*."

Salwa takes Mary by her trembling hand as the *imam* addresses her: "It's so nice to have you here with us, and we know this is a big moment for you. Are you 100% sure you believe in the words you're about to say?" Through her jitters, Mary remembers her deep desire to become Muslim and responds, "Yes, I believe." It has been a journey of years and finally she is here. Mary tells herself not to mess this

---

[1] We have a glossary for all the weird Arabic words that come up.

up.

The *imam* says, "Repeat after me." She fumbles with the words of the *shahada*, foreign and strange on her tongue, but as soon as they fall from her mouth, she feels relief. Suddenly, there is an eruption of emotion around her. She becomes the recipient of tears, hugs, kisses (on both cheeks), nuggets of wisdom that make no sense to her, and of course, some donated clothing and books. She is told she is now a sister to them all. Women who are complete strangers offer her their phone numbers.

A few days, a few weeks, a few months go by and the spiritual high wears off. Reality sets in. No one seems available to answer her questions or to just sit and talk. The questions, concerns, and backlash from friends and family all come flooding in at the same time her new support looks surprisingly scarce. Mary feels at peace in her new faith, but more alone and confused than ever.

---

### In the name of God, the Most Gracious the Most Merciful

How many of us can relate to that experience? It's almost universal, and we say that with true sadness. We come into Islam with such high expectations, and the welcome we receive upon embracing Islam is usually full of fanfare and excitement. But within 5.4 seconds, we feel alone and confused, left to our lonesome to navigate the rocky waters of a world we have very little or no knowledge of.

*The New Muslim's Field Guide* (heretofore known as *The Field Guide,* for short) is the book we wish we had been given by our friends in the *masjid*, right along with the Quran and the *Seerah* and *dua* books. We wrote *The Field Guide* to help prevent that confusion, that overwhelmed-ness, and protect any new Muslim reading this book from disenchantment and embitterment because "[...] Allah intends for you ease, and does not want to make things difficult for you [...]" (Quran 2:185), even if sometimes people make things difficult, intentionally or otherwise.

## WHAT IS A "NEW" MUSLIM?

Conversion to Islam is technically simple. One needs only to say—with firm conviction, in front of witness(es)—the *shahada*, or the declaration of Faith: "I bear witness that there is no god except God, and I bear witness that Muhammad (peace and blessings be upon him- PBUH) is God's final messenger." And just like that, one becomes Muslim! *Allahu Akbar*!, and all that.

However, in *The Field Guide*, we define "new Muslim" a little more broadly than just those who have recently said the *shahada*. The "new Muslim" here can be anyone who is just now starting to learn about their faith or just now beginning to live life as a practicing Muslim (even if they were raised in a Muslim home).

But just because the book addresses new Muslims doesn't mean this book isn't for you. All readers are welcome, whether he or she may be non-Muslim, raised-as-Muslim but just now starting to take their faith seriously, people who are doing research on Western converts to Islam, *masjid* admin, *imams* who want to help the converts in their congregations, friends of new Muslims, or people who want to gift a book to a Muslim—really everyone!

## SOME CHALLENGES NEW MUSLIMS FACE

Converts to Islam are often asked to hold cultural, racial, ethnic, national, political, and post-colonial baggage for everyone, whether they are Western, Eastern, or formerly Christian, Jewish, Sikh, Hindu, etc. It's a big bag and it's hard to carry. But it is thrust upon the convert to Islam because it is thought that we bridge both worlds and are seen as a conduit of sorts, whether or not we welcome the role.

The new Muslim, in particular, is blindsided by the repercussions of all this baggage. He or she often finds him or herself pushed out of "Islamic" spaces because these spaces are often more like ethnic clubs or centers than the *masajid* that they claim to be. And from time to time, the new Muslim (and unexpecting porter) experiences rejection from foreign-born, heritage Muslims who simply cannot separate culture from religion.

Adding insult to injury, the already overburdened new Muslim is often disowned by family and friends because of some ill-informed but well-listened-to media myths. These same battered new Muslims often face discrimination from their own society-at-large due to a growing climate of Islamophobia in the West.

Still, many new Muslims never regret their decision to live Islam and be Muslim. But because of the aforementioned issues, new Muslims, unfortunately, can find themselves going down difficult paths with heavy burdens. With the help and hindrance of zeal and naiveté, many find themselves stumbling or even being tripped on their journey. But have no fear, "[...] for verily, Allah is with those who believe" (Quran 8:19). And "[...] Allah is the ally of the believers." (Quran 3:68)

*The Field Guide* is here to unpack all that baggage

(and more), show the new Muslim where the traps are lain, and teach the new Muslim how best to navigate this path.

WHAT IS *THE FIELD GUIDE* ALL ABOUT?

*The Field Guide* is so much more than a "How-To". It is literally a guide to be taken with the new Muslim into the uncharted fields of their new life. *The Field Guide* will direct the new Muslim through the natural occurrence of identity issues. It will be their companion on the road of intra-Muslim relations. With handy descriptions, it will be here for the new Muslim to browse as they begin the journey into the practice of Islam, directing them in the many skills they need to learn to become savvy, self-possessed Muslim in the modern world.

Furthermore, *The Field Guide* is not a candy-coated pep rally to convince the new Muslim that he or she has made the right decision in converting to Islam. The new Muslim has indeed made the right decision, but we do not wish to indoctrinate them. Quite the opposite. We encourage the new Muslim to question everything.

*The Field Guide* is here to be frank and honest with new Muslims, in hopes that our advice will help in the real world. Things can get real, very fast once one takes *shahada*. And too many heritage Muslims (those Muslims who have been raised in Muslim families) out there—who have all the best intentions at heart— don't understand what that is like and don't have the down to earth, nitty-gritty advice the new Muslim needs for the tough situations he or she may face.

This is the book we wish we were handed on Day One of our conversion to Islam. This kind of guide would have been nice to help us identify what we were encountering. If nothing more, it would have been good to know we were not alone. It is our hope that new and future Muslims will find solace, some guidance, and maybe even some laughter in our advice, experiences, and fumbles.

## WHO ARE THE PUPPET-MASTERS?

We are a couple of American Muslim converts. We are writers, thinkers, ranters, and women who refuse to go into the box that has been built for us. *And we have been where you are.* We have been down the road of what seemed impossible and lived to tell the tale— some of which is hilarious in hindsight, and some of which was brought on by our own making. With our collective experience working in the fields of culture, faith, and politics—as well as our experience dealing with some corrupt co-religionists and some bigoted co-culturalists—we have some hard-earned advice.

It's our hope that you, dear new Muslim, will learn from our mistakes and our sufferings, and maybe choose the better path.

## THERESA WHO?

Theresa Corbin is a French-creole American, writer, editor, up-cycler, and a Muslim convert. She is the author and designer of *The Islamic, Adult Coloring Book*. She is a contributing writer for the internets, specifically Al Jumuah, About Islam, and several other online publications. Her work has also been featured on CNN and Washington Post. Corbin holds a degree in English lit from the University of South Alabama, and has been studying culture, gender issues, Islamic thought, and sectarianism since 1998. She is also the founder and undisputed, lightweight champion of islamwich.com

In 2001, shortly after converting, Corbin delivered a speech about her path to Islam at Louisiana State University's Islam Awareness Week alongside Kareem Abdul-Jabbar (shameless name-dropping, we know), even though she had no clue who this overly-tall man was until after the fact (as she is decidedly not a sports fan). In March of 2015, she was invited to Sheikh Yasir Qadhi's community in Memphis, Tennessee, to deliver a speech about understanding Islam to the Memphis community at large. In December 2015, she travelled to Sydney, Australia to an academic conference where she presented her research into women's rights in relation to Islamophobia.

Corbin's life is constantly changing. At the time of this book's publication, she continues her writing career but no longer indulges comment sections, gives speeches, or does interviews. She does enjoy the white magic of baking, long walks by the bayou, and putting her phone on silent. She enjoys a quiet life with her husband, cultivating a cozy hermitage. But there is no telling what tomorrow will bring.

KAIGHLA WHAT?

Kaighla White, known online as "Kaighla Um Dayo," is a writer and story-teller extraordinaire. Before embracing Islam in 2009, she was an evangelical Christian who attended Lincoln Christian University, majoring in Missions.

Aside from the work she does with Theresa at islamwich.com, she is finishing up her Bachelor's Degree in English Language and Literature from Southern New Hampshire University, expecting to finally graduate in Winter 2018.

Having survived a messy divorce after a miserable

marriage to a Sheikh, lived out in rural Egypt, Kaighla works hard to enlighten Muslim women to their God-given rights and works to alleviate the fears that keep them trapped in oppressive marriages and lifestyles.

Kaighla lives with her children and her newlywed husband in the States, enjoying the green and nature and rain she missed in Egypt. She is also deeply interested in the benefits of mindful meditation as a method of dealing with the stresses of modern life.

Like Theresa, she has left social media in favor of more intimate, authentic connection.

Her greatest passion is sharing the wisdom she garnered across the last 10 years: Life sometimes hands you lemons, but you don't have to be bitter.

### WHERE IT ALL CAME FROM

Like all good and ironic things, the seeds of *The Field Guide* were sewn in the comments of a Facebook post. We—both bloggers, writers, and converts to Islam—expressed a desire to write a blog post about what we wish we had known when we first converted to Islam. Unlike most ideas hatched in the comments section of social media, it actually came to fruition as a set of blog posts on islamwich.com.

We thought it might take up the space of, max, two blog posts. But then it quickly grew into three, and finally ended up being five blog posts and nearly eight podcasts full of fun facts, graphics, anecdotes, and advice. Once all was said and done, we knew that the blog posts, podcasts, and comments were just the tip of the iceberg. We wondered what would happen if we put all this information into one place, like in some sort of collection of paper and glue and binding? What would it be then? A gritty TV crime drama? A stand-up act? Or just a piece of origami?

Maybe, we thought, we could have it professionally printed on smooth, cream-colored paper, then bound behind a beautiful cover (designed by Theresa) using supernatural patience and other such sorcery. And so, *The Field Guide*, the book, was spawned.

But who reads introductions anyway?

# 1- You're Still You:
# And That's a Good Thing

Embracing Islam is surely one of the most life-changing choices you'll ever make. But when the people clear out of the *masjid* and the donated *hijabs/kufis*, Qurans, and pamphlets are in your trunk, you will be sitting there in your car in the same skin in which you walked into the *masjid*.

And this is a very, *very* good thing. Islam did not come to kill your individual identity, but to enrich it. But still, maybe you're not sure what to do from here. There's this overwhelming feeling that big changes are coming into your life, and this is true. But you may also feel that you must make everything about you different from this point forward, and that's *definitely not* true. Your heart is good, and you just want to improve yourself for the pleasure of Allah (SWT). However, before you run away with (or from) yourself, lend us an ear.

We assume that you have some life experience behind you, and those experiences came together in a beautiful painting, with each brushstroke representing life events that have made you uniquely you, and brought you to this place where you have accepted Islam as your way of life.

We are here to tell you: *being you is not a bad thing*. If you take a backward glance at the last couple of months/years leading up to your conversion, you'll probably see in hindsight a series of events or stepping stones. Perhaps some of those life experiences were positive or pleasurable, but we think it's safe to say that many of them were probably painful experiences.

Discomfort is the catalyst of change. Otherwise, you would not have taken steps to find something better, something more meaningful, and something that would change your life for the better. Whatever the case may be, the path to Islam is riddled with opportunities that Allah (SWT) gave you to see that there is nothing and there is no one in life we can ultimately rely on beyond Him. Many times in life our struggles, our losses, and our trials are just Allah's way of calling us back to this ultimate reality.

Our point is that each one of these experiences that you had in your life up to now, including your personality, your previous religious background, and your family dynamics—all these things came together to guide you along your path toward embracing Islam. There is no reason to act as if these things do not matter and cast them aside.

The purpose of Islam is to know peace through knowing God. Of course, as new Muslims, we all have things in our past we would like to forget, whether it's past sins or people who've hurt us along the way. There is nothing wrong with this feeling. A major draw of embracing Islam is the opportunity for a new beginning; a clean slate, as it were.

But starting anew does not mean running away from who you are at your core. It doesn't mean denying the things you have done in your past, or the painful relationships of your past. Every experience you have had in your life can be a lesson and should not be forgotten 'cause we can all use lessons learned in our journeys to come.

Unless there is something in your life right now that is clearly, obviously forbidden (and someone has presented authentic evidence from the Quran and *Sunnah* to prove it), you should not stop doing it just because you embraced Islam. Don't quit your job unless it's literally dealing with *haram* things (and even then, start taking the appropriate steps to securing a new and *halal* job before you walk out). Don't walk away from your family, as it is a serious obligation for the Muslim to maintain family ties. Don't change your name unless it has a bad meaning. Don't stop talking to your non-Muslim friends, though we highly recommend ending any inappropriate relationship(s) with members of the opposite sex. Otherwise, though, don't imagine that Islam forbids you from having non-Muslim friends.

Now, if you have friends who bash Islam or attack you for choosing this religion, or advise you to abandon it or "suffer in eternal hellfire," they aren't very good friends, and you should seriously consider if they are worth keeping in your friend repertoire. Don't throw away your wardrobe. Whether you are a man or a woman, do your best to be modest. Don't feel like you need to wear all black if you're a sister, or a *thobe* if you're a brother. Is it loose? Is it modest? Are all the parts of your body that should be covered, covered? As long as the answer to these questions is "yes," wear it out in public! If the answer is "no," feel free to wear it in the house.

You don't have to learn to speak Arabic or Urdu, friend. It may sound like "Islam-eese" but really, there is nothing holier or better about speaking these languages than speaking your own. Don't sweat learning Arabic right away (except when learning how to pray). Allah (SWT) knows us better than we know our own selves: "And We have already created man and know what his soul whispers to him, and We are closer to him than [his] jugular vein." (Quran 50:16)

God knows what you want to say before you even want to say it. Yes, there are *duas* (supplications in Arabic that the Prophet (PBUH) used to say) and these are great, but the important thing is to speak from your heart. Sure, traditional Quranic Arabic is important to try to learn and to understand so that you can grasp the deep, profound meanings of the Quran that can't be translated fully to another language. But you won't magically be more spiritual if you drop Arabic words here and there. You will surely be more accepted into the Arabic or the South East Asian *masjid* club, but speaking Arabic in your day-to-day life won't enhance your relationship with God in the least.

Don't toss all the foods and drinks you love and replace them with Middle Eastern or Pakistani food and drink. Sure, *falafel* is great, but so are your family's recipes. As long as they don't include pork or alcohol, you are good to go. And if the old recipes you love do happen to contain pork or alcohol, just replace them with a *halal* option. If you are addicted to alcohol (or any other drug or mind-altering substance) you need to start taking steps to recovery. Please don't be embarrassed to seek help if you need it. You are improving yourself and there is NO shame in that.

Are you catching our drift? You. are. a. human. with. an. identity. Let go of this delusion of a brand-spanking new life post-conversion. Yes, many things will change. But you can't escape yourself (even if you want to) by embracing Islam. You will still have the same quirks, the same hardships to overcome, the same strengths and weaknesses, and the same fears and dreams. Allah (SWT) wants you to refine your identity, not toss it in the burn pile.

## TALES FROM THERESA TOWN

It was the year twenty hundred and one. "W"- the second Bush- was in the infancy of his presidency. The founder of Facebook was still in high school. And I had just become a Muslim. Like many of you, I was ready to change. *Everything.* I recall sitting on the floor of my closet sorting through clothes that I felt no longer fit into my Islamic lifestyle. One pile to keep. One pile to trash. *Abayas* and *shalwar khamees* dangled over my head on their hangers as they were spared the chopping block. My roommate's younger sister was in town for a visit and I decided it was a good idea to see if she wanted any of my not-so-modest clothing.

As she dug through my painstakingly procured prior-to-Islam wardrobe, I felt a pang of loss. When she picked up my soft, green baby-T) that encouraged all who read it to "have a whale of a time," I had to leave the room. I had loved that shirt. We had great times at barbeques together. We spent many hours in the library pretending to study. But I thought here was where we had to part ways.

I was wrong, but, after converting to Islam, I treated most of the things in my life the way I treated my wardrobe. I quit my two jobs (one at a newspaper and one in a clothing store), neither of which were anywhere near *haram.* I ignored my non-Muslim friends. I even distanced myself from my family. Once everything and everyone was gone, and all the dust settled, I had no lounging around clothes, I had no connection from my past, and I had a family that was deeply hurt by my distancing.

I realized I was alone with myself and that self was still me, for better or worse. In getting rid of these *halal* things, I had attempted to do the work to become a better person and a good Muslim, but all I had done was remove anything that reminded me of my identity. Guilt and shame followed me for years until I finally faced what I had done and started the work of repairing it.

It was hard work getting back all that I had lost. Some people I could never get back. And I still regret this foolish phase mostly because I hurt a lot of people. But also, because I gave them the idea that embracing Islam meant I had to changed who I am. I was wrong, but it is a hard thing to unteach.

# 2- Culture & Islam

The reality is that many Muslims in the West today are either the children or grandchildren of immigrants, or are immigrants themselves. This means that most converts will be "brought up" in the faith surrounded by people who were generally raised in a culture, at least in their home, that is very different from the culture to which the convert is accustomed.

## CULTURE HAS A PLACE

Before we get into semantics about separating culture from religion, it's important to note: none of us is without a culture. If you've never left your country, your state, or even your hometown; you may have the impression that you and your family and friends–and the way you all do things–are "normal" and everything else is "different." But the reality is that everyone in the world was born and raised in a specific cultural context. And that's not a bad thing.

Allah (SWT) tells us that He made humankind in a huge variety of colors and tribes because he wanted us to know one another:

> O mankind, indeed We have created you from male and female and made you peoples and tribes that you may know one another.

Indeed, the most noble of you in the sight of Allah is the most righteous of you. Indeed, Allah is Knowing and Acquainted. (Quran 49:13)

Islam was not revealed to take away one's culture, whether that culture is found within Muslim-majority countries or not. But, the reality is that there is no culture that perfectly represents the tenets of Islam. Not one. Not even Saudi culture, the home of the *Kaba*. Just as well, culture has a real place within Islam.

There is a concept in Islamic jurisprudence called *urf*, and it roughly translates to "culture." There are many circumstances wherein there is no clear ruling on something and the end determination comes down to the *urf* of the person involved. For example, let's say two Muslims want to have an American-type wedding, with the vows and the walking down the aisle and all that—this is fine! As long as it doesn't violate clear Islamic ruling, there is nothing wrong with keeping a tradition.

## WHY IT MATTERS

Because there is a great chance you will be at least partially surrounded by Muslims who were raised in a different culture, it's extremely important to know, from the start, that just because a heritage Muslim or even a convert from way back tells you something, that doesn't make it true or right in Islam. It is easy to relax and assume that if your average Khadijah or Muhammad say *x* is *haram* or *y* is *halal*, it must certainly be so, because they are heritage Muslims, right? Wrong.

It is of the utmost importance that you, as a new Muslim, build a strong foundation of faith that includes fact-checking sources. Otherwise, it will be very easy for outside forces to shake up your faith later when you come down from the "convert high." We have seen far too many Muslims fall away from the faith because they were bombarded from the outset with not only the huge changes Islam brings, but were shouldered with the gigantic burden of being forced to adopt a foreign culture.

Hear us now: there is no reason you must give up your culture and heritage to embrace Islam. Allah (SWT) created you and placed you within the family and culture wherein you were raised. Unless something in your culture is downright clearly against the Quran and the *Sunnah* of Muhammad (PBUH), there is no reason to give it up.

## SEPARATING THE WHEAT FROM THE CHAFF

But how? How can we come to know the difference between what our Muslim friends tell us is Islam, and what is just their Jordanian, Egyptian, Moroccan, Iranian, Saudi, Pakistani, Indian, or Indonesian culture? Demanding evidence for a ruling is a great way to make sure you aren't being indoctrinated into a culture instead of what you are really trying to do: live Islam. But more than asking for a source, know that "Ok, but why?" is still a valid and important question. Listen, you are an educated, informed, woke human being who has chosen to follow a religion that most of the people in your life are not too gung-ho about. In the 21st-century, Western society, it's more socially acceptable to be an atheist than it is to be a Muslim. There is no way you came to this faith without having a questioning, inquiring, curious mind. Don't throw that away now that you are in the fold of Islam. Your brain and your mindset are what brought you into Islam, and they are necessary for establishing a healthy foundation as a Muslim.

When brother Khalid tells you that *x* is *haram*, ask him why. When sister Mariam tells you that you absolutely must do *y*, ask her for the evidence. When the *imam* of the *masjid* stands at the *minbar* and tells you that you absolutely cannot do *z*, refuse to accept it is inherently true by default just because, hey, he must know what he's talking about to have been given that platform, right? Not always.

Maybe he got that job because he knows the right people, and that is an unfortunate reality. A lot of medical doctors get in the position as *imam* with little to no Islamic knowledge simply because many Middle Easterners and South-East Asians respect medical doctors. Go home, read, read, read, and ask questions if you really want to understand more.

## (Most) Everything is Relative

Maybe you live in a community wherein most Muslims are Somali, or Indian, or Pakistani, or some type of Arab. Each and every one of those cultures is very sure that their particular brand of Islam is the right one, and they will–often with good intentions– pressure you to adopt their way of life, wrapping it in the pretty packaging of THIS IS THE ONLY RIGHT WAY TO BE MUSLIM, THANKS.

Don't buy this.

There is a Muslim culture and it's outlined in the *Sunnah* of our Prophet Muhammad (PBUH). It includes things like not responding to hate with hate, allowing people to believe what they want to believe without pressuring them, being modest in your dress and way of interacting with people, being humble

25

and honest in every circumstance.

But Islam also takes into account cultural standards. For example, the great majority of Arab cultures, as a whole, do not value punctuality. We don't say this as a degradation, but an anthropological observation: there are time-based cultures and there are event-based cultures. So, whereas you and I may look at time as "1 o'clock," other, more event-based cultures may look at time as "around *Dhuhr* prayer." Of course, there were no clocks during Prophet Muhammad's (PBUH) life, so it is likely he lived according to that culture. But, when living in a time-based culture, punctuality is a very serious sign of respect, and perpetual lateness is a very clear sign of personal disregard for the time and energy of others.

As a rule, a Muslim should understand that respecting other people is very important. So, if the people with whom we are interacting view being late as disrespectful, a Muslim should do his level-best to be on time. If the wedding is supposed to start at 7PM, one should do their best to be there at 7PM. But that's in a time-based culture! If you were to show up at 7PM for a "7PM" wedding in an event-based culture like India or Morocco, there is a good chance nothing would even be set up yet. So, the respectful thing to do is to show up when the people who know them better suggest they will actually be ready for the wedding.

Let's look at another common example: wearing shoes in the house. You will hear a very broad range of beliefs on this seemingly irrelevant point, but within that spectrum will be people who insist that it is absolutely *haram* to wear shoes in the house, as well as those who say it's merely a respectful and hygienic thing to remove one's shoes in the house, regardless of religion. It is not actually *haram* to wear shoes in a home, but if that homeowner finds it very gross, or even thinks it is *haram*, it is disrespectful to wear shoes in their house. Thus, wearing shoes in that person's home would be very disliked because doing so would show disrespect.

You get the picture: *culture is relative.* Our perspective of respect, love, and modesty may be just as valid and well-within the realm of acceptable Islam as yours, depending on the culture wherein we reside, and sometimes even depending on the home or family with whom we are living.

Whatever it may seem like, the world's Muslim population is very diverse. According to Pew Research Center, only 20% of the world's Muslim population is Arab.[2] Muslims are spread out all over the world.

So even though the predominant face of the Muslims in Western media is a bearded Arab man screaming in Arabic, that's just not an accurate representation (just as most things in Western media do not represent reality). Just because the Indo-Paki or Arab culture seems predominant in the minds of most people as "Muslim culture," this does not make it so. Try telling a Muslim in China or Uzbekistan that their Muslim culture is "wrong" because it is very, very different than that of Egypt or Bangladesh.

CANDID KAIGHLA

As soon as I converted, I was bombarded by people telling me I needed to change this or stop that or dress like this. I was blessed to have been donated a mix of Indo-Paki and Arab clothes from women in

---

[2] Lipka, Michael. "Muslims and Islam: Key findings in the U.S. and around the world." *Pew Research Center*. Online.

the community, but I wish I could have had access to more American-style modest clothing and scarves.

I have always had an obsession with other cultures and I embrace new ones easily. But I have a habit of totally disappearing into that new culture, and when the culture is mixed in with some Islam, it becomes a sick cycle of rebellion and guilt when I wake up and realize, "Hey, I am still the same girl inside I was when I was 14 and 17 and 21 and this doesn't look or sound like me."

I remember a few months after I had married my first husband (an Egyptian), I came back home to Chicago to visit some friends. I was dressed in an *abaya* and a big scarf and I felt proud to be presented to my friends as "the *Sheikh's* wife." We sat down in the same room we used to joke and laugh and be loud in, but I was sitting quietly in a chair while they sat on the floor, as was our old custom.

All I wanted was for it to end so I could be done trying to act a certain way, all because my then-husband spent so much time telling me how much my mannerisms and ways of dealing with people were incorrect. When in reality, they were just contrary to his culture.

My Muslim, Indo-Paki friends were clearly picking up on my vibes and were extremely uncomfortable themselves. One of them muttered to the other under her breath (when she thought I could not hear), "*Oh my God. She is just so Arab now.*"

I cried on my way home because I felt proud to be more "'Muslim", with my "Muslim" clothes and my *mashaAllah*s and *alhamdulillah*s and *inshaAllah*s and *habibti*s all timely placed. But to everyone else, it was obvious I was trying to fit into a role I wasn't meant for, and it wasn't God who expected it of me.

Later, my then-husband and I moved to Egypt so

that he could be fair to his other wife there (whom I knew nothing about when I married him). Suddenly, I was surrounded by an entire population of people in their village who thought I was a Martian. They treated me like an outsider, and were deeply suspicious of my dedication to both Islam and my then-husband.

Any time I did anything differently than they were accustomed to, I was told it was wrong in Islam. Didn't put six layers of clothing on my children in 80-degree weather? I was a bad mom and *haram alayk*, they said. Didn't celebrate Prophet Muhammad's birthday with them? I was too strict in my practice. Insisted on wearing *hijab* in front of his cousins? I was not friendly enough. Smiled at the beautiful day or something my kids said or did outside? I was inviting flirtation because "good Muslim women don't smile in front of other men." And the list goes on.

Ultimately, I came to a point wherein I had had enough and decided that unless something was definitely *haram* with evidence, I was going to live my life in the way that I saw fit. I did my best to be culturally sensitive, of course, but I stopped curbing my entire personality for their sakes.

Unfortunately, because of some key aspects of the culture, dishonesty and a lack of punctuality are fairly standard among people in rural Egypt. Of course, they wouldn't call themselves dishonest; they'd say it was just a "white lie." This tendency to allow "white lies" in one's life was stretched to the extreme when men hid secret wives from their families in order to "avoid hurting them." One could almost never rely on someone to do what they said, when they said. And the old Arab adage *"inshaAllah, bukrah"* (God-willing, tomorrow) was dropped so often when the speaker really meant to say either "God-willing,

29

tomorrow" or "Yeah, that's never gonna happen" or "Maybe if I have time" or "Not unless God forces me" or "in a few days" and anything in between.

These tendencies drove me batty, and quickly. More than dealing with being told I was wrong all the time, it was harder and harder to see Muslims living in ways that are against the spirit of Islam in what I thought was a "Muslim country." The moral of the story is: Islam is a religion, not a culture, and it knows no nationality nor bends itself to fit into one.

# Beyond Culture: Women's Rights in Islam

There is so much said about women's rights on both sides of the fence. Non-Muslims who have little to no knowledge of Islam–and see the sometimes-rampant misogynistic actions of Muslims–claim that women have no rights in Islam. While Muslims claim that women do have rights in Islam, sometimes Muslims confuse cultural dictates with Islam and take those Islamic rights away from women. Much of what we know or are taught about Islam in the West comes from strict, patriarchal societies where the lines of what is part of a patriarchal culture and what is actually Islam are blurred. Unfortunately for women, this means we must fight for our Islamic rights that patriarchy, at times, encroaches upon. But, fear not, we can arm ourselves with knowledge.

Islam has a very skeletal, societal structure when it comes to gender roles. There are zero *hadith* that say a woman has to stay at home and cook and clean. There is no Quranic verse that says a woman cannot work outside of her home and make money if she wants to. Our foremothers were scholars, farmers, merchants, managers of marketplaces, doctors, nurses, teachers, soldiers, CEOs of non-profits, business owners and bosses, mothers, and homemakers, and so much more.

Take Khadija (may Allah be pleased with her), the Prophet's first wife, for example. She was a very successful business owner, a mother to many, and she ran a charity out of her home for the poor—Muslim and non-Muslim alike—in Mecca. She was the one who proposed marriage to the Prophet (PBUH) and she was also the first to accept the message of Islam when the Prophet himself was in shock after the first revelation.

Or consider Aisha (may Allah be pleased with her). She was one of the greatest scholars of Islam. Much of what we know about our religion comes from her. She stood up to men of great stature and put them in their place with her significant knowledge when they were straight-up wrong. She had no children, but took in girls and molded the next generation of female scholars.

## WOMEN AS EQUAL

For the majority of human history, women have been thought of as secondary to men. Aristotle once wrote that "the female is, as it were, a deformed male."[3] Not cool, Aristotle! Not. Cool.

When the religion of Islam was revealed to Prophet Muhammad (PBUH), it marked the first time in human history when woman was not defined as a lesser creature than man. The Prophet (PBUH) said,

---

[3] Aristotle. *The Generation of Animals.*

"Women are the twin halves of men." (Narrated in *Abu Dawood* and *Tirmidhi*) A woman is not thought of as only a wife, sister, and daughter. Her personhood does not hinge on her relation to others. She is person in her own right. An Individual. She doesn't have to be bonded with a man or try to imitate men just to garner respect. She was not assigned worth based on her appearance or appeal. She was and is on the same footing as man.

In large pockets of human history, women were even thought not to have souls. Islam shuts the door on that kind of thinking. According to the Quran, men and women were created from the same soul, neither male nor female having any superiority based on gender:

> O mankind, fear your Lord, who created you from one soul and created from it its mate and dispersed from both of them many men and women. And fear Allah, through whom you ask one another, and the wombs. Indeed, Allah is ever, over you, an Observer. (Quran 4:1)

In many other faiths women are seen as sirens and even the origin of evil. In Christianity, for example, when Eve (from Adam and Eve) was left holding the blame for "original sin", and for a long time it was thought that all women inherited Eve's "wicked" ways.

In Islam, there is no such thing as original sin. We do not inherit sins. Each individual soul is responsible for his or her own actions and rewarded equally. "[...] No person earns any (sin) except against himself (or herself only), and no bearer of burdens shall bear the burden of another [...]" (Quran 6:164) And, according to Islam, Adam and Eve were both held equally responsible for disobeying Allah (SWT). And they were both forgiven for their transgression.

Gender has no bearing on our relationship with God. Men are not closer to Allah (SWT) than women are, or vice versa. The only distinction between people is based on our own work to be nearer to Allah, our efforts to become among the righteous. And we all have equal opportunity to achieve righteousness. Allah says in the Quran:

> Surely, for men who submit to God and for women who submit to God, for believing men and for believing women, for devout men and devout women, for truthful men and truthful women, for steadfast men and steadfast women, for humble men and humble women, for charitable men and charitable women, for fasting men and fasting women, for men who guard their chastity and women who guard their chastity, for men who remember Allah much and for women who remember Allah much; for all of them Allah has prepared forgiveness and a mighty reward. (Quran 33:35)

In 7th century Arabia, after Islam was revealed, women enjoyed full legal independence. Women were given the basic right to education; to own property; to buy, sell, trade; to own a business/to work; to move freely throughout society; to choose whom and when she would be married IF she would be married, and to facilitate her own divorce if she so chooses. All these rights were protected under Islamic law. The status of Muslim women, at this time in history, was unheard of in many societies until modern times. So, remember, when countries, cultures, or individuals take away these rights from women, it is in direct contradiction to Islam and not because of it.

As a Muslim woman, you are required to pray, fast, give in charity, perform *Hajj*, and affirm the statement of faith. You are required to always strive to be the best you that you can be. You are required to seek an education. The Prophet (PBUH) said, "Seeking knowledge is mandatory for every believer." (Narrated in *Ibn Majah*) You are also required to show respect to those in your family and show kindness and mercy to the rest of humankind. These are your responsibilities as a human. They are the same responsibilities as any other Muslim:

> The believers, men and women, are protectors, one of another: they enjoin what is just, and forbid what is evil, they observe regular prayers, practice regular charity, and obey Allah and His Messenger. On them will Allah pour His Mercy: for Allah is Exalted in power, Wise. (Quran 9:71)

If anyone tells you that women have to go through a man to get to God, that women are responsible for the sins of others, or that they can't have agency in their own lives, know that they are coming from a place of patriarchal impulse, regressive culture, and/or a severely misguided, misogynistic reading of Islam.

# 3- *What's in a Name?*

There is no universal requirement to change your name when you convert to Islam. None. At all. Yes, there *are* some situations wherein changing your name becomes incumbent upon you: if your name has a meaning which contradicts the message of Islam, for example, you must change it. We'll give a few examples in a moment, but first, let's delve into why and how Muslims have gotten the impression that changing one's name upon conversion is required.

## EARLY MUSLIMS AND NAME CHANGES

One of the major reasons Muslims believe that a new Muslim must change his or her name is because of the several people who changed their name when they became Muslim during the life of Prophet Muhammad (PBUH). One such person was 'Aasiyah, one of the daughters of a companion of Muhammad named 'Umar. "Aasiyah" means "disobedient." Because of this, the Prophet renamed her "Jameelah," which means "beautiful." (Narrated in *Muslim*)

However, there is a precedent set for *not* changing one's name, too. Ibn al-Musayyab said that his father came to the Prophet (PBUH) and he asked him, "What is your name?"

"Hazn (meaning rough)," he said.

Prophet Muhammad said, "You are Sahl (meaning easy)."

Rather than accepting this injunction from the Prophet of God, he replied, "I will not change the name that my father gave to me." (Narrated in *Bukhari*)

Had changing one's name just because one enters Islam been obligatory, surely Prophet Muhammad (PBUH) would have rebuked this man and insisted he change his name. However, since his name didn't have a meaning directly against Islam and its message, or one that was offensive, he did not press the issue. And his name even had a sort of less-than-beautiful meaning.

### HONORING YOUR PARENTS

One of the most agreed-upon tenets of Islam is the command to honor and respect your parents. Allah (SWT) says in the Quran:

> And your Lord has decreed that you not worship except Him, and to parents, good treatment. Whether one or both of them reach old age [while] with you, say not to them [so much as] *'uff* [i.e., an expression of irritation or disapproval] and do not repel them, but speak to them a noble word. And lower to them the wing of humility out of mercy and say: 'My Lord! Have mercy upon them as they brought me up [when I was] small.' (Quran 17:23-24)

Part of honoring your parents is recognizing that they chose that name for you, often after pouring over baby name books and asking members of their family for their opinions for literally months. If you have children, think about how you would feel if they came home one day and told you they had decided their name wasn't good enough because "God doesn't like it." You'd feel hurt, offended, and confused, for one thing, and then you would be seriously put-off by whatever crazy religion your child decided to follow that commands him or her to cut ties with the name he/she have carried all her/his life.

### TAKING MY HUSBAND'S LAST NAME?

A note to you sisters who are planning on changing your name when you marry your husband: don't. The tradition of changing one's name after marriage to one's husband comes from a practice of ancient Christian Europe where it was believed that the woman getting married goes from being property of her father to property of her husband. Daughters, wives, women are not property.[4]

Prophet Muhammad (PBUH) said, "Whoever claims knowingly to belong to someone other than his father will be denied Paradise." (Narrated in *Bukhari* and *Muslim*) See, Islamically, the last name (surname, family name) you use denotes what family or tribe you belong to, the one you were born into, and the one your father was born into. Claiming you are from the Zoubi or Kilani or Johnson or Frasier or Khan or Ahmed family because you married a man who is, is completely stepping on the face of your father's family, your own family, who raised you.

Now, we understand this can be hard for some sisters. Many of us as young girls sat and wrote our name next to a prospective husband's name when

[4] Gilbert, Elizabeth. *Committed: A Skeptic Makes Peace with Marriage.* New York: Viking Press, 2010. Print.

beginning a relationship with him, just to see how it would sound and look should we marry him. We understand this can sometimes be something hard to swallow because of our culture, one based primarily on European Christian customs, but when one has to choose between Islam and culture, Islam must prevail, regardless of where you come from.

### WHEN YOU *DO* NEED TO CHANGE YOUR NAME

Let's say your name is "Christina" or "Christian," you should probably change your name because it means "Christ-worshipper" and you're not. If your name means "I am God," you should prolly change your name because you are not God—obviously. If your name means "killer" or "destruction," for example (we can't actually find any names with this meaning, but hey, stranger names have happened), you should change your name because you are neither a killer, nor a bringer of destruction.

**Some not-so-good reasons to change your name:**

1. You want to enhance your apparent Muslim identity by adopting an Arabic name. An Arabic name does not enhance your Muslim identity. You can and should strive to be a better Muslim through your intentions and actions. Besides, Arab does not equal Muslim.

2. You want to distance yourself from your old identity. You should not shed your old identity. Just improve upon it. You will always be you. You are uniquely made up of your experiences, style, personality, and quirks. Embrace that and incorporate the endlessly beneficial teachings of the Prophet Muhammad (PBUH) into who you are.

But why not keep your name and make it a Muslim name? If your name is Bob and you are a Muslim, then by the transitive property, Bob is now a Muslim name. *Voila!* You are creating a bridge between the West and Islam. And that is pretty cool.

## CANDID KAIGHLA

Since my first day in kindergarten, I have had a love/hate (mostly hate) relationship with my name. "Kaighla" is pronounced "kay-la," but my young mother felt like being cheeky and novel, so she threw a few extra letters in there for good measure.

Every year, for the first few days of school, I would be able to predict with almost 100% accuracy when my name would be called in class. For one thing, my last name falls in the back of the alphabet, so I knew I would come toward the end. But the real give-away was the look on the teacher's face: without fail, they would squint their eyes, pull the attendance sheet closer to their face, and begin with, "hmmm ... k ... ka"

"Present," I'd say. "And it's Kaighla. Like Kay-la, just spelled differently."

If anyone made fun of the spelling (and they often did), I would laugh along with them, and the jokes about my mom's poor choice were abundant. I spent the greater part of my youth hating my name and hating the way no one could pronounce it, and I always fantasized about growing up and changing my name to something more beautiful, more elegant, like Elizabeth or Katherine.

However, in the past seven years, a new feeling has emerged within me, one of affection and even a sense of offense when someone criticizes my name.

It began as soon as I said *shahada*, and it usually went something like this:

"Oh, sister! *Asalamu Alaikum*! It's so nice to see a new Muslim, *mashaAllah*! And what is your name?"

"*Walaikum Asalam*! My name is Kaighla."

*nervous laughter or smug glare* "Oh ... ha ha ha ... hmmm ... no, I meant your Muslim name, since you're Muslim now, I mean."

Of course, they are always expecting an Arab name, because Arab = Muslim, right? Wrong.

At the beginning of my life as a Muslim, I agreed with them and assured them I was searching for a good name, at which point they would inevitably make several suggestions, always including Aisha, Khadijah, and Fatima, of course. However, there came a time when I learned the truth: since my name doesn't have a bad meaning, and since my mother chose it for me, for better or worse, it's my name.

# Speaking of Names: Convert or Revert?

The term "revert" has been popularized in Muslim communities over the last couple decades and has been internalized by those Muslims who were not born into Muslim families i.e. heritage Muslims. Calling Muslim converts "reverts" comes from the belief in Islam that all human beings are born with an innate nature called *fitra*.

The *fitra* is basic human nature that includes belief in God, His oneness, and knowing the basic difference between right and wrong. And so, it is thought that the *fitra*, or default setting of human beings, makes everyone born a Muslim. But as the child grows, their family, culture, and society can lead the child's natural inclinations, beliefs, and behaviors away from their Muslim nature (or improve upon it depending upon the environment a child is in).

So, when someone comes to Islam later in life, it is thought that they are coming back to it or *reverting* to their nature, their *fitra* as a Muslim. And therefore, some call new Muslims "reverts." You can feel free to call yourself whatever you want: convert, revert, warrior princess, boss man, as long as you are comfortable with it. But we use the term "convert" in this book for a few reasons:

For one to revert, one must first convert to something else. And for one to convert, there must be a choice–a cognizant decision. For us, and many people, there was no such conversion process. We, Theresa and Kaighla, had no choice in the matter of becoming Christian. We were raised in the Christian faith, practicing American culture, and taught the beliefs of those around us.

And for most people; our parents, culture, and society indoctrinate us into a faith, tradition, culture, and belief system that may be different than the true nature of the human being. Nowhere does the child have a choice in this process- a crucial component of converting. This is to say that we did not first, by choice, leave our nature or *fitra* and choose something other than Islam. We did not convert to another faith as children because indoctrination is not the same as conversion.

When we became adults, with the ability to think for ourselves and examine the world around us, we left the faith we were raised in. And we examined the practices of our culture and the beliefs of those around us, taking the good and leaving the bad. We consider this a true conversion because it was made once we were old enough to reason and make that

41

choice for ourselves.

Each person needs to make the same choice in order to consider him/herself a Muslim, or a true member of any faith. Once an adult, it is up to each person to examine what they have been taught. Each person should think, examine, and choose for him or herself.

But the whole premise of the "revert" philosophy leads one to believe that every Muslim born into a Muslim family is left or encouraged to grow up on his or her natural state or *fitra*, and will arrive in adulthood still upon that true nature of the human being. Sadly, this is not always true.

The assumption is that only non-Muslim parents make their child depart from their natural state. But there are, without a doubt, parents who call themselves Muslims who teach their children immoral and corrupt behavior, whether they attribute it to their faith, culture, or personal belief, it makes no difference.

The child born into a Muslim family is just as easily subjected to corrupt behavior and teachings as the child born into a non-Muslim family. The choice is up to each person as they come into maturity to continue the traditions of their upbringing without examining whether they are good and just, or to truly think for themselves and find the truth in the world-the truth that God has sent to us. This applies not only to those raised as non-Muslims, but also to those raised in Muslim families.

SO, WHAT DOES IT MATTER?

It really doesn't matter. We only discuss it here so that you know what's what, why some people use the term "revert," and why we are using the term "convert."

If you prefer one term over the other, go for it! We support you. Also, we don't care what you call us (just don't call us late to *iftar*, please and thank you).

# 4- All in the (Non-Muslim) Family

Sure, all this advice is great. But how in the heck are you going to tell your family that you are now a Mozzzlim!? If you already have, then you are ahead of the game. But if you haven't yet, we know that the thought of telling the people you love anything big and probably something they won't agree with is like ... coming out of the closet ... as a Muslim.

To take the pressure off you, we have put together a letter for your family (see below). You can tweak it however you like but we feel it (briefly) covers all the bases and can be a tool to open dialogue between you and your loved ones. So, feel free to copy and hand out this letter or, even better, hand over the book to your loved ones.


DEAR FAMILY,

So, you have a new Muslim in the family, and you may be wondering, "Where did I go wrong?" Or maybe you are thinking you have lost this person forever. Know that your new Muslim family member is still here, still loves you, and is still him or herself. Take a deep breath. It's all going to be OK.

Before you get upset about a member of your family converting to Islam, why not understand what that really means beyond what the media claims?

Islamic teachings are not alien. Islam is one of the world's largest monotheistic religions. Muslims believe in one God, the same God that Christians and Jews believe created everything. It's just that in Arabic, the word for God is "Allah," the same word that Arab Christians and Jews use.

Muslims believe in the Prophets, from the first man (Adam) to Moses, Abraham, Jesus, and Muhammad (peace and blessings be upon them all). Muslims believe that each Prophet came with the same message: we are supposed to worship the One and Only true God and to be good, kind, compassionate, and truthful people. Islam isn't anything new or malevolent. Forget what you heard on the news.

This info might be a surprise because of all the negative things about Islam you have heard from various sources. However, consider that the media's job is to make money, and nothing sells better than fear, and lately, outrage seems to be selling. Often, this means that the media focuses on stories of the small percent of "Muslims" who seek to achieve political goals by un-Islamic means. That is not to say that these groups should be ignored or discounted, but to say that the groups that cause terror and destruction are a small fraction of Muslims who act in contradiction to Islam but get all the media attention. The media largely ignores the overwhelming majority of Muslims who want peace and who speak out against these small groups.

Don't assume that the new Muslim in the family wants to run off and join a terrorist organization. In all likelihood, they will want to stop these groups from their destructive path and from giving all Muslims a bad name. While the world tunes in to news about self-proclaimed Islamic groups and the various human rights violations which some majority-Muslim countries commit, understand that just because some Muslims do it does not make it Islamic.

Muslim behavior isn't always Islamic behavior. This is a very important distinction to make.

Groups like ISIS act in direct contradiction to Islam. One example of this is forcing people to convert to Islam. The Quran (the Muslims' holy book) says in chapter 2, verse 256, that: "There is no compulsion in religion." And this principle is reaffirmed in chapter 109:6 where it states: "For you is your religion, and for me is my religion." Islamically speaking, each person has the freedom to choose the religion they wish to observe. And that is a right that all must respect. Also, when majority-Muslim countries strip women of their basic rights, they are acting in direct contradiction to the rights and freedoms the Prophet Muhammad ensured for Muslim women over 1,400 years ago.

One example that is often cited as evidence that women in Muslim countries aren't free is the fact that up until very recently, women in Saudi Arabia were not even allowed to drive. However, in the time of the Prophet Muhammad, women were free to ride animals, today's equivalent to driving. Islamically speaking, human rights—including women's rights like the right to drive, to work, to self-determination, or the right to obtain an education—are protected in Islam. The Prophet Muhammad (peace be upon him) said: "The seeking of knowledge is obligatory for every Muslim." (Narrated in *Ibn Majah*) And God, in the Quran, says:

O mankind, indeed We have created you from male and female and made you peoples and tribes that you may know one another. Indeed, the most noble of you in the sight of Allah is the most righteous of you. Indeed, Allah is Knowing and Acquainted. (Quran 49:13)

Unfortunately, some Muslims are not good examples of what Islam is. And the new Muslim in your family likely understands the difference between Muslims' actions and Islamic teachings. If he or she didn't, it is not likely that he or she would have converted to Islam in the first place.

It's also not about culture. Another widely-held misconception that may make you wonder why your family member chose Islam is that Islam is about being Middle Eastern. Islam is not about any one culture, nor is it specifically for any one group of people. In fact, only around 20% of the world's Muslims come from the Middle East.

And just like there are Christians, Jews, Buddhists, and people of other religions from many different cultures around the world, there are Muslims from every culture and every country. Your newly-converted family member will not have to abandon their identity. Islam doesn't dictate that they become part of another culture.

Your loved one is also not brainwashed. As the number of Muslim converts grow in the West, there is a lot of speculation as to why so many people are choosing Islam. Some say that Muslim converts have been brainwashed. This is a superficial and erroneous answer to a complex question. There are as many reasons people come to Islam as there are Muslim converts. Not one of them is brainwashed. This is because brainwashing always involves coercion or the breakdown of mental faculties. And saying the *shahada* in Islam (the action that makes someone a Muslim) is like signing a legal document or giving testimony in court under oath. The testament of faith in Islam, like the legal document or court testimony, is only considered admissible if the one testifying has not been coerced and is free from mental defect. These two components—coercion and/or mental incapacity—are key components in brainwashing and consequently invalidate acceptance of faith.

Each person that chooses Islam for his or her life has had to wade through many misconceptions and myths about the faith themselves. They may have had, at one point or another, many of the same questions you have about Islam. Ask the new Muslim in your family why he or she chose Islam for his or her life. Let your loved one tell you why. The answer might surprise you.

TALES FROM THERESA TOWN

I sweated telling my family about my conversion to Islam. Like hardcore freaked out at the thought of it. This thought/fear kept me from saying my *shahada* for over a year. To psych myself up to do it, I kept thinking, "They might not like it. They might even hate me for it, but they will get over it in time and come to accept me." I was right.

It has been 17 years now (as of 2018) and my family and friends who are still around are super cool with my choice of Islam. They have taken the time to learn about Islam. They warn me if pork or alcohol is in something. They defend Islam to others. And they even throw me *Eid* parties! But the road to this point wasn't always easy.

For the most part, when I broke the news to my

family members, they were super cool and laid back about my conversion. Most of them now have confessed that they thought it was a phase I was going through. But there were a couple of integral people in my life who were so freaked that they swore to never speak to me again.

Sadly, one family member died before we got the chance to come to a place of understanding. And the other made good on her word not to speak with me. I know that this reaction had nothing to do with me and everything to do with her fear and ignorance. This person just felt it was best to protect herself from whatever she thought might happen to me. And that's ok too. She finally came around and we have a pretty healthy relationship now.

If someone in your life does happen to disown you or cut off ties with you, especially a family member, be patient. He/she might just need time to wrap their mind around it. Many people don't do well with change. A lot of people know very little about the truth of Islam and might freak out thinking you are joining a death cult. Be patient. Don't write them off. Show them mercy and don't go bad-mouthing them to everyone. Leave the door open. They will come to realize you are still you and you still love them.

# 5- *What a Muslim Believes: The Six Pillars of Faith*

You—you beautiful, brand new Muslim—have ignored what the media has told you. You sought the truth about God. You understood your Creator's message through time and prophets. You realized all are welcome, be they young, old, black, white, Arab, Asian, American, or European. You recognized that Islam is for all people, for all time. And you accepted it in your heart. Congrats! You're kinda awesome.

We're guessing you've probably been told about the five pillars of Islam. And by now you probably have realized that these five pillars of Islam are action-based—they are what the Muslim does. But we both know belief comes before action.

And guess what? Allah (SWT) knows that is how the human operates, too. Not a shocker. After all, Allah created us that way. And that is why for the first 10 years of revelation, the theme of Allah's message focused on belief. Once belief was firm in the hearts of the Muslims at the time of the Prophet Muhammad (PBUH), then the revelation focused more heavily on the ins and outs of living Islam.

Aisha, one of the wives of Prophet Muhammad (PBUH), who was a wise woman and force to be reckoned with, said:

> If the first thing to be revealed was: 'Do not drink alcoholic drinks,' people would have said, 'We will never leave alcoholic drinks,' and

if there had been revealed, 'Do not commit illegal sexual intercourse,' they would have said, 'We will never give up illegal sexual intercourse.' (Narrated in *Bukhari*)

She was right. People don't just follow orders for no reason. If the companions did not love Allah (SWT) and believe in His truth first, they would have never given up all the things that hurt us and therefore lead us away from Allah.

A Muslim believes in six pillars of faith (*iman*). *Iman* has been defined by this conversation between the Prophet Muhammad (PBUH) and the angel Gabriel:

> Once, when the angel Gabriel came to Muhammad (PBUH), he said to the Prophet: 'Inform me about *iman* [faith].' And Prophet Muhammad said, 'It is that you believe in Allah and His angels and His Books and His Messengers and in the Last Day, and in *qadr* [fate], both in its good and in its evil aspects.' He [Gabriel] said, 'You have spoken truly'. (Narrated in *Bukhari* and *Muslim*)

## 1-Belief in the Oneness of God (*Tawheed*)

**Say, 'He is *Allah*, [who is] One. *Allah*, the Eternal Refuge. He neither begets nor is born. Nor is there to Him any equivalent.'"**
**(Quran 112:1-4)**

A Muslim believes in one, *uno, un, wahid*, ONE God- it's a strict monotheism thing, otherwise known as *tawheed*. It is the belief in God's absolute oneness. It's that first part of the thing you said that made you a Muslim, the *shahada*: "I bear witness that there is no god except God."

Allah (SWT) is the same Creator and sustainer of the universe that sent the Ten Commandments. Allah is the same God that sent Jesus (Isa- PBUH) as a Prophet and allowed him to perform miracles. Allah is the same God that sent all the prophets to guide us to the worship of Him alone, without partner. We don't need to travel to outer space (even though that's cool if you want to), or go on some psychedelic trip (that is decidedly less cool), or find some fossil of a guru to understand the meaning of life. Muslims know that the purpose of life is singular: to worship Allah alone. In effect, worshiping God, drawing nearer to Him and knowing Him, is the path to true peace. That is all. Worshiping God and knowing peace through Him is the meaning of life. But that doesn't mean that we are only supposed to spend our time in prayer. Most things we do can be a form of worship if you do them to know Allah, to come closer to Him, and find peace through Him.

The Muslim believes in specific things about Allah (SWT): He alone is worthy of worship, and none besides Him is worthy of worship. He has no partner, no begotten son. Nothing is hidden from Him. He is the owner of power. He has created all that is in existence and all that will ever exist. He gives life and causes death. He gives sustenance to all creation. He does not eat, drink, or sleep. He is eternal. He was not created. He does not have any parents, spouses, or offspring. All depend on Him, and He depends on none. Nobody resembles Allah, and He resembles nothing. He is free from all faults.

It's a lot of stuff to remember, but that is why you bought this book, so you can come back to it as a guide when in the field.

**Side note**: The pronoun, "He," is used as a placeholder for "Allah," but Allah (SWT) does not have a gender. Being male or female implies that you are in need of the opposite sex. Allah is in need of nothing. We only use "He" because English has failed us by not producing a gender-neutral pronoun besides the degrading "it."

**Bonus side note**: Sometimes when the Quran is interpreted in English, "We" is used when Allah speaks of Himself. The "royal 'We'" is being employed in these instances. This is the use of a plural pronoun to refer to a single person holding a high office, and what higher office is there than Creator of all? This does not mean that Allah thinks of Himself as a plurality. It's just a weird formality of archaic English.

## 2-Belief in all of Allah's (SWT) Messengers

**"Then We revealed to you [Muhammad], 'Follow the creed of Abraham, a man of pure faith who was not an idolater.'"**
**(Quran 16:123)**

This is that second part of that thing you said that made you a Muslim, the *shahada*- "[...] I bear witness that Muhammad (PBUH) is God's final messenger."

Islam is not a new religion. Each prophet—Moses (Musa), Abraham (Ibrahim), Job (Ayyub), David (Dawud), Jesus (Isa), and many more, as well as the last Prophet, Muhammad, peace be upon them (PBUT)—came with the same message: *Worship God alone and follow his prophets as the best of examples.*

The Muslim believes that a prophet was sent to every nation in the history of humankind to convey this message to their people. Allah (SWT) sent these messengers for us to follow as examples of how best to worship Him, how best to live a life free from harming ourselves and others, a life that is at peace with the creation and the Creator. And the last in this lineage of prophets was Muhammad (PBUH).

## 3-Belief in the Holy Books

**"We sent Isa, son of Mary, in their footsteps, to confirm the Torah that had been sent before him: We gave him the Gospel with guidance, light, and confirmation of the Torah already revealed–a guide and lesson for those who take heed of God. [...] We sent to you [Muhammad] the Scripture with the truth, confirming the Scriptures that came before it, and with final authority over them [...]"**
**(Quran 5:46-48)**

The Muslim believes in five books that are mentioned in the Quran:
- o *As-Suhuf* (The Scrolls)- of Ibrahim and Musa.
- o *At-Taurat* (The Torah)- revealed to Musa.
- o *Az-Zaboor* (The Psalms)- a holy book given to Dawud.
- o *Al-Injeel* (The Gospel)- revealed to Isa.
- o *Al-Quran*- the final revelation revealed to Prophet Muhammad.

The Quran and Prophet Muhammad (PBUH) confirm what has come before in the Torah and the Bible and they have brought the same message (worship the one and only God and follow His messengers) that all previous prophets came with, even if some of the laws may have been different.

While the Scrolls of Ibrahim have been totally lost, the Psalms, the Torah, and parts of the Gospel have not. You might have heard of them. Today we know of them as the Torah and the Bible. But–and this is a big but—these holy books are *not* in their original state. Ask any Bible scholar where the original Torah, Psalms, and Gospel are and he or she will tell you that we do not have the originals. Muslims (and all people who study scriptural history) believe that some verses from these books have been added, some have been taken out, some have been completely changed, and their sources cannot be traced back to the prophets to whom they were revealed.

This may seem like a huge bummer because something so important as the infinite wisdom of Allah (SWT) has been tampered with by the finite ideas and words of man. But fear not! That is why we still have the Quran, and Allah has promised that He will protect it and keep it in its original state, exactly as it was revealed to Prophet Muhammad: "We [Allah] have, without doubt, sent down the Reminder [i.e. the Quran]; and We will assuredly guard it [from corruption]." (Quran 15:9)

We still have it both in the hearts and minds of millions of Muslims and in written form in the Arabic in which it was revealed. The memorization of the Quran by Muslims since its revelation has protected the written form from being altered in any way.

### 4-Belief in the Angels (*Malaika*)

**"Everyone has a succession of angels in front of him and behind him, guarding him by Allah's command [...]."**
**(Quran 13:11)**

When you read this, you may have imagined the cherubs of your childhood. Nope! These are not the little, fat babies with wings you were thinking of. Angels are not divine, nor do they share in Allah's

(SWT) divinity. Muslims believe in angels who, unlike us, do not have free will.

Despite what the Bible claims, angels cannot "fall from grace," and Satan (*Shaytan, Iblis*) was not an angel before his fall, but a *Jinn* (another form of creation, a huge topic we don't have the space to cover in this book). Angels are in complete obedience to Allah and have no choice in this. Angel *Jibril* (Gabriel) delivered the message of Allah to all the messengers. There are angels who write down our deeds. There are angels who will question us in our grave, and so on.

Why do we believe in angels? Because the Creator of you and me and the stars and galaxies said that He created angels. Moreover, the belief in Angels is central to Islam because of the fact that God revealed his Truth not to Muhammad (PBUH) himself, but to Gabriel (Jibril) who then delivered it to Muhammad (PBUH). If we didn't believe in the existence and inherent goodness of Angels, we would have a hard time believing the claim that they brought the message of God.

## 5- Belief in The Day of Judgment
### (*Yawm Al-Qiyamah*)

"He asks, 'When is the Day of Resurrection?' So, when vision is dazzled and the moon darkens and the sun and the moon are joined, man will say on that Day, 'Where is the [place of] escape?' No! There is no refuge. To your Lord, that Day, is the [place of] permanence. Man will be informed that Day of what he sent ahead and kept back."
(Quran 75:6-13)

The day of Resurrection, as seen in Christianity

and Judaism, is something we have in common because, remember, we have the same God who sent the same message, some of which survived in these respective religions. But you knew that already. This is the day we are all heading towards. It is the day we will, as the name suggests, be judged by Allah (SWT). This day gives context to our lives and our actions. We are all working toward–or are heedless of–this day when the sum of our beliefs, intentions, and actions will either be rewarded or punished.

## 6-Belief in Predestination (*Qadr*)

**"And with Him are the keys of the unseen; none knows them except Him. And He knows what is on the land and in the sea. Not a leaf falls but that He knows it. And no grain is there within the darknesses of the earth and no moist or dry [thing] but that it is [written] in a clear record."**
**(Quran 6:59)**

This ain't your momma's Protestant predestination. Predestination, fate, or *qadr*, in Islamic thought has everything to do with Allah (SWT) being All-Aware. Whereas we humans have a linear understanding of reality, Allah, The Limitless Creator of humans and time, is not constricted by the same linear timeline. Allah has created the future and understands intimately what it holds, just as He has created our past and present. Even though Allah knows and has willed what will happen in the future, we still have free will in the present.

Some of the wisdom of *qadr* in Islam is that it gives us confidence that what comes to us would never have missed us and what misses us would never have reached us. We don't have to waste time crying over spilt milk; it was never meant for us. But since *we* do not know the future, we still have to put forth the effort in the now. All we have is now, our intentions, and our effort.

This is a bare-bones summary of the six pillars of *iman*. Continue to learn the ins and outs of these pillars. A great resource for learning more is *Essentials of Islamic Faith* by Suhaib Webb.

# 6- *What A Muslim Does: The Five Pillars of Islam*

Welcome to the world of action. If the pillars of Islam and *Iman* were movies, the six pillars of *iman* would be a romance movie—minus the gross smooching and whatnot—because the six pillars of *iman* are all about feelings, trust, and belief. But the five pillars of Islam would be an action movie because they are all about, yes, that's right, actions.

Simply put, the five pillars of Islam are what the Muslim does. This is an extremely important component in refining the heart and drawing closer to Allah (SWT). But it is not because Allah needs our actions; it is because we need these actions to keep faith in our hearts and peace in our lives. It's kinda like exercise for the soul.

You may have noticed in your life that some days you feel like doing all the things and other days getting out of bed is not an option. This fluctuation in mood and energy levels is similar to the fluctuation of faith: it is not a fixed thing.[5] Some days you will feel very close to Allah (SWT) and you want to do all

---

[5] "It is He who sent down tranquility into the hearts of the believers that they would increase in faith along with their [present] faith [...]" (Quran 48:4)

the extra stuff to get closer to Him. Some days you don't feel so enthusiastic and you have to drag yourself to do the minimum. This is the fluctuation of *iman*, and it's totally ok, human, and even normal. So, don't freak if this happens to you.

The five pillars of Islam are the minimum acts required from the Muslim to maintain a baseline level of *iman* and connection with Allah (SWT). Like the minimum exercise required to keep your muscles from atrophy, the five pillars are what your soul needs to stay healthy. There are extra things we can do as Muslims, like giving extra in charity, or praying extra (*Sunnah*) prayers, or performing *Umrah* (non-obligatory Pilgrimage), etc., but we must keep up with these five things at the very least.

A MUSLIM PRACTICES THE FIVE PILLARS OF ISLAM:

"Once when the angel Gabriel came to Muhammad (PBUH) he said to the Prophet: 'Inform me about Islam.' The Messenger of Allah said, 'Islam is that you should testify that there is no deity except Allah [SWT] and that Muhammad is His Messenger, that you should perform *salah*, pay the *zakat*, fast during *Ramadan*, and perform *Hajj* to the House [the *Kaba*], if you are able to do so.'" (Narrated in *Bukhari* and *Muslim*)

1-Testimony of Faith (*Shahada*)

"Say [O Muhammad], 'I am no more than a human, like you; being inspired to me that your god is but one God. The one who hopes to meet his Lord shall work good deeds and never associate any others while in the act of worshiping his Lord.'" (Quran 18:110)

"I bear witness that there is no god except God. And I bear witness that Muhammad (PBUH) is God's final messenger." When said in Arabic, it sounds something like this: "Ash-Hadu Ina La E-LaHa illa Allah wa Ash-Hadu Ina Muhammad Rasoul Allah."

To become a Muslim, you must complete this first pillar in front of witnesses and truly believe it, being free of coercion and of sound mind. The *shahada* is an action because when you say it and believe it, you must then live it. To start with, you learn what it means to worship only one God and follow God's messenger (PBUH). You are learning what that means now by reading this book, so you are on the right track. Good on ya, mate!

It may seem easy at first to only worship one God. Sure, you probably didn't bow to statues or believe in Zeus, or what have you, before Islam, and you probably don't now. But putting anything before Allah (SWT) in your life constitutes worship. And anything worshipped turns that thing into a false god; that's how it works. And there are so many traps that we can fall into, slipping into worship of other things.

Whatever we obsess about, whatever we would do *anything* for, even the *haram*, is what we worship; whether it is a person, money, sex, shopping, love, status, our own desires, or our own limited logic/reason. It is our nature to worship. We seek it out, and often, we seek it in the wrong things.

All these worldly things cannot help us without the Creator's permission. You will always be let-down by worshipping other than Allah (SWT). That is not to say that we can't like money, love people, enjoy sex, and be fond of shopping, etc. As long as these things are liked and loved in a *halal* way, you're good to go. This is to say that we cannot put these likes and loves

61

and our desires in God's place, as something we live for, as the thing we seek out before all else.

This is something all people who consider themselves Muslims must be conscious of at all times. The Muslim leaves behind all other forms of worship and all other false gods, and worships only the one true God. For more about this subject, check out Yasmin Mogahed's *Reclaim your Heart*. It will walk you through the ins and outs of how to take back your heart from the creation and devote it to the One that made everything you love and desire.

The second part of the *shahada* is declaring that you believe in God's final messenger, Prophet Muhammad (PBUH). Allah (SWT) sent us an example of how it looks when a human person does as Allah wishes. By saying it, and believing it, we have to then live it out by following the Prophet's example. This need for a role model to follow is also part of our nature. When we do not follow God's guidance through Prophet Muhammad, we find bad substitutes to follow. You might have noticed this followship most-pronounced in teenagers. They cling to celebrities. They know EVERYTHING about their favorite performing artist. And then they follow their way (*sunnah*) to a "T".

Beyond our teenage years, we continue to follow celebrities—people who have not been guided to the truth. We follow stars who fade and become a source of ridicule in a few short years. We follow fashionistas whose style will be outdated in a few months. We follow public figures, politicians, and scientists who will eventually be disproven or exposed in some way. But a Muslim leaves behind all other examples and follows the perfect example of the Prophet of *Allah* (PBUH).

Note: A Muslim should never blindly follow

anything or anyone, even if she/he is told it is from the messenger of Allah (PBUH). A Muslim should always verify his/her sources and the context in which the example was said or done.

## 2-Prayer (*Salah*)

**"Guard strictly the *salah*, especially the middle *salah*. And stand before Allah with obedience."**
**(Quran 2:238)**

After you declare your faith with the *shahada* and start implementing this belief in your life, the next action you should start incorporating into your life is the ritual prayer, or *salah*. Prayer in Islam is a little different than in other faith traditions. To people of many other faiths or those coming to Islam from another faith tradition, a "prayer" is usually considered to be a request of God. In Islam, this *is* a kind of prayer, called a supplication or *dua*. But the prayer we are talking about here, the prayer that is a pillar of Islam and required of us, is called the *salah*.

This pillar is an act of worship (and *dua*, or supplication, can be included as a part of this act of worship, but can also be done outside of *salah*) that the Muslim does five times a day. It involves movements of the body, including standing, bowing, prostrating, and sitting. Five times a day you leave behind whatever you are doing to commune with God, to connect without intercession to the One who created you and all that exists.

Each of the five daily prayers needs to be performed in its specific allotted time frame. And each prayer is named after the time in which it is performed.

1-Pre-dawn, in Arabic called *Fajr*

2-Noon, in Arabic called *Dhuhr*

3-Afternoon, in Arabic called *Asr*

4-Sunset, in Arabic called *Maghrib*

5-Night, in Arabic called *Isha*

But because we are in constant motion in relation to the sun—you know, astronomy and all that—these times are always changing throughout the year. When the days are short, the prayers are closer together. When the days are long, the prayers are further apart. Your location on the earth also plays a part in determining prayer times. But don't stress out about getting your astronomical charts and abacuses out and calculating the correct times to pray. You can just go to islamicfinder.org, enter your city, and the experts have already calculated when prayer time starts, and there are plenty of apps for both Android and iOS that will even remind you when it's time to pray.

But the prayer does not need to be performed the exact minute the prayer time comes in. There is a window of time you have to pray that prayer. Similarly, the prayer time does not always expire when the next prayer time comes in. Sometimes prayer time ends well before the next prayer comes in. *Fajr* ends at sunrise; *Dhuhr* ends at *Asr*; *Asr* ends at *Maghrib*; *Maghrib* ends when the light has left the sky in the west; and *Isha* ends half way between the start of *Isha* and the start of *Fajr* the next day. There are some scholarly differences of opinions about the end times of prayers, but to play it safe, pray as soon as you are able when the prayer time begins.

In order to pray, you must learn some Arabic, specifically the first chapter of the Quran called "The Opening" or *Al-Fatiha*. It sounds like a lot when we call it a chapter (*surah*), but it is only seven short verses (*ayat*), so don't break out in a cold sweat just

yet. It sounds like this:
Bismillaahir Rahmaanir Raheem
Alhamdu lillaahi Rabbil 'aalameen
Ar-Rahmaanir-Raheem
Maaliki Yawmid-Deen
Iyyaaka na'budu wa Iyyaaka nasta'een
Ihdinas-Siraatal-Mustaqeem
Siraatal-lazeena an'amta 'alaihim
ghayril-maghdoobi
'alaihim wa lad-daaalleen

It means this: In the name of Allah, the Entirely Merciful, the Especially Merciful. All praise is due to Allah, Lord of the worlds - The Entirely Merciful, the Especially Merciful, Sovereign of the Day of Recompense. It is You we worship and You we ask for help. Guide us to the straight path. The path of those upon whom You have bestowed favor, not of those who have evoked [Your] anger or of those who are astray.

This chapter is the first chapter of the Quran and the first chapter you should learn of the Quran. Read it. Learn to say it in Arabic (see the "sounds like" part above and start sounding it out). Study all that it means. When you pray five times a day, you catch on to the sounds of the Arabic pretty quickly. But always remember you must keep in mind the meaning, otherwise you are just spouting gibberish you don't understand or believe in and there is no benefit in that. Learn more about what is required before and during prayer (*salah*). YouTube is a great resource for new Muslims learning how to pray.

Allah (SWT) knows how difficult or easy learning *salah* is for you to learn and incorporate into your life. He does not expect perfection from you in your first *salah*, or even your hundredth; He does expect

65

you to try. So, take your time and understand what you are doing. Do your best and always try to keep improving your *salah*. While *salah* is pretty easy to get the hang of, the perfect *salah* is a lifelong pursuit that even those who learned to pray as children are still trying to implement. A Muslim leaves behind the day-to-day activities five times a day to reconnect with Allah in *salah*. *Salah* is so important that we dedicated the entire next chapter to it.

### 3-Almsgiving- Charity (*zakat*)

**"Truly, those who believe and do righteous deeds, and perform *salah*, and give *zakat*, they will have their reward with their Lord. On them shall be no fear, nor shall they grieve."**
**(Quran 2:277)**

The next thing we, as Muslims, do is give to the poor from our wealth–if we have any. There are two kinds of this obligatory almsgiving, or *zakat*, that a Muslim is required to give.

*Zakat al Mal* is 2.5% or 1/40th of any wealth you have accumulated above a set amount (see quote below). It is to be paid yearly and is to be given to someone in need. According to Dr. Muhammad Ahmad Al-Musayyar, Professor of Islamic Creed at Al-Azhar University (a very, very old Islamic university in Egypt), *Zakat al Mal* is:

> [...] To be paid when the savings reach the prescribed value, which is equal to 20 *mithqals* of gold [$3,403.78 US as of 2016] and 200 dirhams of silver [$300.48 US]. It can be paid at any time of the year, as long as the minimum amount remains in one's possession for one year.

*Zakat al Fitr* is $10 (what today equals three kilos of wheat, barley, dates, or rice - i.e. a staple food) which the father or husband is required to pay for each person in the family (those he is in charge of providing for—his kids and spouse, not extended family). *Zakat al Fitr* is to be given to someone in need before going to the prayer on *Eid* (celebration) after the month of fasting (*Ramadan*- the next pillar to be discussed). Again, that $10 is to be paid for each person in your family before *Eid* prayer, if you can afford it, to a needy person.

Yes, *zakat* involves math. But Allah (SWT) does not expect you to be a mathematician. You can defer this math—and specifically the extra math-iness of *Zakat al Mal*—to the scholars or those who are in charge of collecting *zakat*.

*Zakat* can be given directly to those in need. Or, if you do not know someone in need, you can give your *zakat* to your local *masjid* for the admin to distribute to those in need. It's important to understand that *zakat* is not for the *masjid* itself. This is not a like a tithe paid to the church. *Zakat* is specifically for equitable distribution of wealth and for the care of those who have need of it. If you do wish to give to the *masjid*, this is another form of charity (*sadaqah*) that is not obligatory but considered a very good deed.

If you do not have any savings, money to give at *Eid*, or are yourself in need, you are excused from this pillar. In fact, it is a tradition that the *masjid*, or local Muslim community, give *zakat* to the new Muslim to make the transition to Islam easier for them. If you are in need of help, do not hesitate to go to your local *masjid*. The *zakat* is your right and the community's obligation to you. A Muslim parts with a portion of his or her wealth seeking Allah (SWT) above all else.

## 4-Fasting (*Sawm*)

**"O you who have believed, decreed upon you is fasting as it was decreed upon those before you that you may become righteous."**
**(Quran 2:183)**

The only time fasting is required of the Muslim is during the month of *Ramadan*. That's right: you'll be fasting for a month. But, before you freak and think you can't handle it, fasting in Islam is not as hard as you may think. It's not like a juice fast where you only drink juice for days on end (tried it. hated it.). It's also not an impossible, no-carb diet.

Fasting in Islam requires that you do not drink or eat from sunup to sundown. No food or drink during daylight hours means that you get to have a breakfast before and a dinner after you fast, or a breakfast after you break your fast and a dinner before you fast, or snack and an eleven-zees in the PM and a lunch at midnight. However you wanna play it as long as you abstain from food and drink (and intercourse with your spouse and sins you would normally stay away from) during the daylight.

These meals before and after fasting are, in fact, highly recommended (if not required), and the breaking of the fast in the evening is often done in gatherings (*Iftar*) at the *masjid*. Afterwards, much merriment is made and then some extra praying called *taraweeh*.

Fasting can be difficult at first when you are not used to the stamina and stomach restriction it requires. With a burger for a dollar available on almost every corner, what Westerner is used to actively *not* eating? At first, you may look at all the people fasting around you and think you are the only one who can't hang with it. But it gets easier. Your stomach shrinks. You start to feel less weighed down. You gain some stamina. And fasting even becomes a pleasure.

Most Muslims look forward to the month of fasting because it is not just about not eating; it is also a time of great spiritual growth, celebration, and community building. You will be surprised how much you start looking forward to the month of fasting and miss it when it is gone when you put your heart into it and make the most of the holy month.

However, not everyone can or is expected to fast. You must be a conscious, healthy adult, free from mental or physical handicap for fasting to be required of you. If you get temporarily sick, you do not have to fast those days you are under the weather (to be made up after *Ramadan* when you are all better). If you suffer from diabetes, an eating disorder, or any illness that affects the way you eat, you must consult your doctor before fasting. Also, if you are travelling, you have the choice to fast or to make it up after *Ramadan*. If you have a chronic illness that would be exacerbated if you were to fast, you are excused from fasting. However, you have to feed poor people instead (ask your local *imam* or person of knowledge how much and how long you have to do this for).

Specifically for the sisters: when you are pregnant or breastfeeding, fasting is not required. If you are menstruating or having postpartum bleeding, you cannot fast, and will have to make up those days you missed by fasting sometime after *Ramadan*. The principle is that if fasting will do damage to your physical health, stop doing it.

A Muslim leaves behind food and drink, feeding instead the soul and growing in *iman* and love of Allah (SWT).

## 5-Pilgrimage to Mecca (*Hajj*)

"And [mention] when We made the House a place of return for the people and [a place of] security. And take, [O believers], from the standing place of Abraham a place of prayer. And We charged Abraham and Ishmael, [saying], 'Purify My House for those who perform Tawaf [circumambulation] and those who are staying [there] for worship and those who bow and prostrate [in prayer].'"
(Quran 2:125)

*"Hajj"* is an Arabic word for pilgrimage. The non-obligatory Pilgrimage is called *Umrah*. Pilgrimage is not a popular concept in modern Western religious traditions, but to have some point of reference that is commonly known (to lit majors and nerds) in the Western conscious, you can think about the pilgrimage in "The Canterbury Tales," where pilgrims are travelling together from London to Canterbury to visit the shrine of Saint Thomas Becket at Canterbury Cathedral.

However, *Hajj* is still vastly different from "The Canterbury Tales" because pilgrimage in Islam is only done to worship Allah (SWT), seeking Him alone. A Muslim would consider a Canterbury-type pilgrimage a kind of *shirk* (associating partners with God), but it is still a journey for religious reasons making it a pilgrimage. But enough about Chaucer.

In Islam the *Hajj* is a journey to Mecca, Saudi Arabia to the *Kaba*. The *Kaba* is a central point of orientation for the Muslim. It is the direction in which we pray, not a building to worship but a unifying directionality. The *Kaba* was the first house of worship of Allah. It was built by Prophet Ibrahim and his son Ismael (Ishmael, PBUT).

*Hajj* to the *Kaba* in Mecca is a religious tradition started by Prophet Abraham. The rituals in this act of worship also come from Hajar's (Hagar) trials when she was left in the desert in the site where the *Kaba* was to be built by Abraham (PBUH). Over time, the *Hajj* of Abraham was corrupted and the pagan Arabs in pre-Islamic times used the ritual to worship idols and promote trade. It was reestablished as a monotheistic devotion by Prophet Muhammad (PBUH).

Every year the *Hajj* begins on the 8th of the month called *Dhu'l-Hijjah* and lasts for five days. *Dhu'l-Hijjah*, which essentially translates to "the month of Pilgrimage," is the last month of the Islamic calendar. *Hajj* is to be performed at least once by every healthy, adult Muslim who has the financial capability. A Muslim leaves behind her/his home and comfort and travels to the first place of worship built by Abraham to become closer to Allah (SWT).

There are 11 basic rites of *Hajj*:

1.  **Intention**

The pilgrim makes his or her intentions for *Hajj* and enters a sacred state called *ihram* by ritual washing and the crossing of the Pilgrimage boundary. Men must be wearing a special clothing called *ihram*.

2.  *Tawaf* **of Arrival**

When the pilgrim arrives in Mecca he/she proceeds to circle the *Kaba* seven times, counter-clockwise. This is called *tawaf* or circumambulation.

71

After completing *tawaf*, the pilgrim performs two units of prayer.

↓

### 3. *Sa'y* al-Safa and al-Marwa

After *tawaf* and prayer, the pilgrim proceeds to the hills of al-Safa and al-Marwa where he/she will run the distance between them seven times, as Hajar did when she was left in the desert with her child, Ismael (PBUT).

↓

### 4. Mina

Pilgrims proceed to Mina where they spend the night in tents.

↓

### 5. Mount Arafat

Pilgrims proceed to Mount Arafat after pre-dawn prayer (*Fajr*). On Mount Arafat, pilgrims are encouraged to read Quran, perform *salah*, and make *dua* to Allah (SWT) for forgiveness from noon to sunset. This is the place where Prophet Muhammad (PBUH) gave his last sermon.

↓

### 6. Muzdalifah

After the sun sets, pilgrims proceed to Muzdalifah (an open, level plain that lies just southeast of Mina on the route between Mina and Arafat) and pray the evening (*Maghrib*) and night (*Isha*) prayers, and spend the night there.

↓

### 7. Stoning the Pillars

After the pre-dawn prayer (*Fajr*) the following day, pilgrims return to Mina. When pilgrims reach the pillars called *Jamarat* in Mina, they throw seven stones at each pillar. This symbolizes the three locations where Abraham pelted Satan with stones when he tried to dissuade him from sacrificing his son Ismael (PBUT).

↓
## 8. Shaving
After throwing stones, male pilgrims shave or shorten their hair. Female pilgrims cut only a small part of their hair (time for bangs/fringe, ladies).

↓
## 9. Tawaf
Pilgrims return to Mecca to perform *tawaf* as they did upon arrival.

↓
## 10. Return to Mina
Pilgrims return to Mina where they reside for three days, each day throwing stones at the pillars that symbolize Satan.

↓
## 11. Farewell *Tawaf*
When the pilgrim accomplishes all the rites and he/she wants to leave Mecca, he/she should perform the *tawaf* of farewell, perform two units of prayer, and then drink *Zamzam* (water from the well of *Zamzam*) asking Allah (SWT) for acceptance and forgiveness.

There are signposts on the road to *Hajj* explaining what to do and plenty of people (literally millions) doing what you should be doing. So, you can just follow them. But also, there are tons of in-depth guides to *Hajj* that you can find online.

Whether we are leaving behind worship of false deities to worship Allah (SWT) alone, leaving behind our day-to-day lives to pray, or leaving behind food and sex when we are fasting, etc., all of the pillars are designed to put the life of this world in a secondary position. We leave the things our bodies desire in order to strengthen our soul, our *iman*, and by doing so, we remind ourselves of what is lasting, and we draw closer to Allah.

Check out *Being Muslim: A Practical Guide* by Asad Tarsin. It goes into much more detail about the ins and outs of practicing these five pillars, and it is complete with pictures!

# 7- Run to Prayer

**W**ithout a moment's hesitation, we can say that prayer is the foundation upon which your entire life as a Muslim is built. If you do not establish a healthy connection with God through the ritual five-times-daily prayers, your life as a Muslim will be shaky and punctuated with emptiness. At the core of all of this is one resounding fact: Islam is a bridge between you and God, not an end in and of itself. Prayer is a five-times-daily journey on that bridge.

The Prophet (PBUH) said, "The first matter that the slave will be brought to account for on the Day of Judgment is the prayer. If it is sound, then the rest of his deeds will be sound. And if it is bad, then the rest of his deeds will be bad." (Narrated in *Tabarani*)

He also said:

> Allah has obligated five prayers. Whoever excellently performs their ablutions, prays them in their proper times, completes their bows, prostrations and *khushu`* [*khushu`* in the prayer is where the person's heart is attuned to the prayer i.e. you are focused] has a promise from Allah that He will forgive him. And whoever does not do that has no promise from Allah. He may either forgive him or punish him. (Narrated in *Malik, Ahmad, Abu Dawud, Nasa'i*, and others)

And for these reasons, we say, run to prayer.[6] The entire reason we make sure to do what is required of us and we avoid what is *haram* is because we want to be near God. If we are living life as a Muslim with any goal beyond pleasing Allah (SWT) so that we can be near Him, we need to check our *niyah* (our intentions) and set ourselves straight.

Why do we wear *hijab*? To obey Allah's (SWT) command and draw nearer to Him. He created us and He knows what is good and what is bad for the well-being of our souls. Why do we avoid *haram*? To obey Allah and draw nearer to Him. Why do we wake up at the crack of dawn every day, day in and day out to pray? Because God has personally invited us to a conversation with Him.

Allah (SWT) loves to hear from us, and He loves it when we seek Him out. Allah says:

> And when My servants ask you concerning Me, then surely, I am very near; I answer the prayer of the supplicant when he calls on Me, so they should answer My call and believe in Me that they may walk in the right way. (Quran 2:186)

While we advise you, dear new Muslim, to take your time and take things slowly, in this chapter, we want to advise you with the utmost passion to run to the prayer. Establishing a healthy prayer habit is the surest, strongest way to ensure your relationship with Allah (SWT).

---

[6] We don't literally mean that you should run to your prayer rug every time it's time to pray. We mean this in the sense that you should be quick to start learning and making prayer a habit. The Prophet (PBUH) said, "When the prayer is held, do not come to it running. Come to it walking. You must be tranquil. Pray what you catch and complete what you miss." (Narrated in *Bukhari*)

When we say "prayer" we are not referring to what you may have been doing all your life whenever you wanted to thank God or when something was bothering you and you needed His help. We do that too, but it's called *dua* (supplication) and it's a spontaneous thing we can do and should do whenever we want to connect with God.

This chapter is about *salah*, which is the Arabic word for the five-times-daily prayers we are commanded to perform by God in the Quran. He says:

> Recite that which has been revealed to you of the Book, and perform *salah*. Verily, *salah* prevents from lewdness and evils. And indeed, the remembrance of Allah (by you) is greatest. And Allah knows what you do. (Quran 29:45)

*Salah* is a prayer with pre-chosen words and body movements which all the Prophets (PBUT) have been doing since the beginning of human creation. We know how to do it and what to say because we know what Muhammad (PBUH) used to say and do. We pray these prayers, five times a day, both because they are mentioned in the Quran, and because we know, from the *Sunnah*, that Prophet Muhammad (PBUH) prayed these prayers at these times each day.

## PROOF FROM QURAN AND *SUNNAH*

Believe it or not, the five daily prayers were not required at first. It was not until around the year 620 CE when Prophet Muhammad (PBUH) was given direct guidance from Allah in the actual Heavens (during something called *Isra* and *Miraj*) when Allah (SWT) took him up to teach us to pray. On his way back down through the heavens, he ran into Prophet Musa (PBUH) himself who had some advice:

> Then Allah revealed what He revealed to me, and enjoined fifty prayers on me every day and night. I came back down to Musa (PBUH) and he said: 'What did your Lord enjoin upon your *ummah*?' I said: 'Fifty prayers.' He said: 'Go back to your Lord and ask Him to reduce it […]' I kept going back and forth between my Lord, may He be blessed and exalted, and Musa (PBUH), until He said: 'O Muhammad, they are five prayers each day and night, for every prayer there will be a tenfold (reward), and that is [the reward of] fifty prayers.' (Narrated in *Bukhari* and *Muslim*)

Thank God that Prophet Musa (PBUH) was there to lay some wisdom down on Prophet Muhammad (PBUH), otherwise we may be praying 50 times a day, friends. In His infinite mercy and love for us, Allah gave us a way to connect with him that wasn't too much, and balance is the name of the game in Islam.

Also, Jaabir ibn 'Abdullah (a companion of the Prophet, may Allah be pleased with him) said:

> Jibril came to the Prophet (PBUH) when the sun had passed its zenith and said: 'Get up, O Muhammad.' That was when the sun had passed the meridian. Then he waited until the (length of) a man's shadow was equal to his height, then he came to him for *Asr* and said: 'Get up, O Muhammad, and pray *Asr*.' Then he waited until the sun set, then he came to him and said: 'Get up and pray *Maghrib*.' So, he got up and prayed it when the sun had set fully. Then he waited until the twilight had disappeared, then he came and said: 'Get up and pray *Isha*', so he got up and prayed it […].

(Narrated in *Nasai'i*)

## ALL THE PROPHETS PRAYED

Even though the formal ritual of praying five times a day wasn't established until just before the migration of the Muslims from Mecca to Medina, we know that all the Prophets (PBUT) prayed in the same way that Muhammad (PBUH) prayed. We have a record of Isa (PBUH), for example, saying:

> He said: 'I am the servant of Allah, He has given me the Book and made me a prophet. He has made me blessed wherever I am and directed me to do *salah* and give the alms as long as I live.' (Quran 19:30-31)

We know that Ibrahim begged God to save his wife Hajar and their son Ismael (PBUT), and mentioned prayer specifically:

> Our Lord, I have settled some of my descendants in an uncultivated valley near Your sacred House [the *Kaba*], our Lord, that they may establish prayer. So, make hearts among the people incline toward them and provide for them from the fruits that they might be grateful. (Quran 14:37)

As far as how they prayed, Allah (SWT) tells us in the Quran:

> [...] And We charged Abraham and Ishmael, [saying], 'Purify My House for those who perform *tawaf* (encircling of the *Kaba*) and those who are staying [there] for worship and those who bow and prostrate [in prayer].' (Quran 2:125)

## A SACRED DIALOGUE

Prayer is not a monologue where we are speaking out into the black abyss and hoping someone receives our message and responds. No, prayer is an actual dialogue between a Muslim and his or her Lord. God tells us that He hears us and responds to us when we pray the *salah*. There is an incredibly moving *hadith qudsi* wherein we learn that God is interacting with us step-by-step after each part of the prayer. Prophet Muhammad (PBUH) said that Allah (SWT) said:

'I have divided *salah* [*Surah al Fatiha*] between Myself and between My servant in two halves and My servant shall have what he asks for.'

So, when a person says, 'All praise belongs to Allah, the *Rabb* [Lord] of the universe', Allah (SWT) says, 'My Servant has praised Me.'

When he says, 'The Most Compassionate, the Most Merciful', Allah (SWT) says, 'My servant has extolled Me.'

When he says, 'The Master of the Day of Judgement', Allah (SWT) says, 'My servant has glorified Me.'

When he says, 'You Alone do we worship and You Alone do we ask for help', Allah (SWT) says, 'This is between Me and My slave and My servant will have what he asks for.'

When he says, 'Guide us to the straight path, the path of those whom You have favored and not the path of those with whom You are angry, nor the path of those who have gone astray', Allah (SWT) says, 'This is for My servant and My servant shall have what he asks for.' (Narrated in *Muslim* and *Nasa'i*)

Let that fact weigh on you for a moment: God hears you, and God responds, right then, on the spot.

This is an issue all of us have faced as new Muslims who do not speak Arabic. Why on earth would Allah (SWT) have made humankind so diverse, with so many languages, and then require that we speak to Him five times a day in just one language? Isn't this unfair?

The answer to that question lies in the question itself: Allah (SWT) did make people in so many different varieties, speaking so many different languages, and in an effort to unify us Muslims as one body, He gave us a pre-set list of prayers to recite in a pre-set language, so that we would feel connected to one another at the very least in *salah*.

## MAKING WUDU & GHUSL

*Wudu* is a state of ritual purity. It is accomplished through the ritual cleansing of the hands, face, nose, mouth, forearms, head, and feet with running water. It is performed after using the restroom, farting, or vomiting, in order to remove impurities before prayer. Before we pray any prayer (the ritual *salah* type), we must make sure we are in a state of *wudu*.

This may seem excessive, and it may make you worry for your water bill and/or the lack of running water in some places, but never fear! There is always a way to make *wudu*. Let's say you are out camping, for example: pour clean water from a bottle and then it's technically running! Let's say you are in a desert

81

and there is no water at all nearby. First: hurry and find some drinking water because ... life.

Then, if there isn't enough water left, you are allowed to use dust/sand/earth to wipe over your face and hands. This way of performing *wudu* is called *tayammum*. Allah (SWT) mentions it in the Quran, "[...] and [if] you find no water, then perform tayammum with clean earth and rub therewith your faces and hands [...]" (Quran 5:6) It's also important to know that Prophet Muhammad (PBUH) never wasted water and used remarkably little to get the job done.

Another important thing to know about *wudu* is that in order to actually be in a state of *wudu*, you must make sure you clean your private parts very well after using the bathroom, using water and toilet paper is best, but not necessary. In case you worry about needing to make *wudu* while on the go, keep a small water bottle in your purse/bag/car/what have you.

Lastly, you cannot be in a state of *wudu* (minor purity) for prayer if you are not in a state of major purity (*ghusl*). What this means, in the crudest terms, is that if you have had an orgasm in any situation awake or asleep (like if you've had a wet dream), or any type of sexual contact with another human being whether or not it led to orgasm, you must take a full bath, or make *ghusl*, to attain a state of major purity.

This just means that you clean off your private area in the shower, preferably with soap, then make *wudu*, and then ensure that your entire body has been covered in the running water, starting with your right side and turning to the left. There are differences of opinion among the many schools of thought on exactly how to make *ghusl*, but all of them contain the basic requirement discussed above.

You may be asking yourself *why on Earth are there*

*so many details*? We must always remember that one of the major parts of Islamic manners is cleanliness. But more than this, making sure you are clean and presentable for prayer gets you in the right state of mind. When you actively prepare yourself for prayer, you are mindfully getting your heart ready to face God. Would you go to a meeting with a King, Queen, or President looking shabby and smelling like last night's dinner? Of course not. How much more do we owe God our dedication to manners and respect?

### DETERMINING THE PRAYER DIRECTION

Now that you have made *wudu* (and *ghusl*, if need be), you are ready to pray. First things first: make sure you know the right direction, facing the *Kaba*, to pray. But what if you don't know the right direction? There are many, many apps to direct you to the *qibla* (the direction of prayer-facing the *Kaba*), both for Android, iOS, and PCs. If you are reading this book in some sort of post-apocalyptic world where these technologies no longer exist, you will need to learn how to determine directionality via celestial bodies anyway, but in the case of *salah* your best guess will do in a pinch.

### BUT WHY ALL THE MOVEMENT?

Another point to ponder are the various positions in which we pray. Each of them is symbolic of our attitude toward God in that moment. We begin the prayer standing upright (assuming one is able). [7] We

---

[7] If you are so sick, injured, or tired that you are not capable of standing at this point in the prayer, then you can sit or lie down, depending on your capability.

stand upright in respect of Allah (SWT), just as we would stand in front of a king or dignitary. But we stand with our head bowed in reverence of the intense reality that The Master of the UNIVERSE wants to hear from us and even *requires* that we have a conversation with Him five times a day.

After we have said *al-Fatiha* (along with some non-obligatory *dua*), we bow at the waist, straightening our back and placing our hands on our knees in the position of *ruku*. This is an act of humility, showing Allah (SWT) our sincere belief that He deserves our full submission. Then, in the *ruku* position, we say any one of various *dua*, including but not limited to: "*Subhaana Rabbiy al-'Adheem,*" which means: "How Perfect is my Lord, the Supreme." (Narrated in *Ahmad* and *Abu Dawud*)

After having completed the *ruku*, we stand again once more, then we come down into prostration, putting our forehead, nose, hands, knees, and toes on the ground in what is the nearest we will ever be to our Lord in this life, in a position called *sujood*. Prophet Muhammad (PBUH) told us, "The closest that a servant is to his Lord is when he is in prostration." (Narrated in *Muslim*)

In *sujood*, we say a specific *dua*, such as, "*Subhan Rabbi al Aaala,*" which means: "Glory be to Allah My Lord, the Most High," or "*Rabbi ighfirlee,*" which means: "Oh my Lord, forgive me!" While still in this position of *sujood*, we can make *dua*, asking Allah (SWT) for anything, sharing our pain and troubles with Him, and seeking peace in knowing He is near and answering us.

We want to encourage you that in *sujood*, you may speak to Allah in your mother tongue. Please don't let anyone tell you that you are not allowed to speak any language you feel comfortable speaking during *dua* in *sujood.*

Then, we sit back on our heels and ask Allah for forgiveness (saying *"Rabbi ighfirlee")* and fall again on our faces (gently, now—no need for a broken nose). Then, we stand and start again from the beginning, as many times as is required by that prayer (which you can learn about in the glossary and in one of the many suggested readings we share at the end of the book). Each of these positions serves to remind us in every way possible that we are humble humans, creations of a Divine and totally Powerful Creator, on whom we depend for everything, including inner peace.

## MISSING PRAYERS AND MAKING THEM UP

You can find out the exact times for each prayer by using an app like Muslim Pro, or visiting islamicfinder.org and searching your location. But what if you miss a prayer? This could be an entire book in and of itself, and it probably is somewhere out there. Here, we will just touch on a few important points.

The general rule of thumb is that a Muslim who is not—a.) on her period, b.) bleeding post-birth, c.) so near death they cannot even wiggle their finger to imitate the positions their body would be making in prayer—must pray every prayer, on time.

Busy and running around? Find time to pray. At work and your boss won't give you space or time to pray? Sue him! Just kidding, but really, seek out legal help because this is your right if you are living in America and many other Western countries. So tired and warm in your bed you just cannot possibly wake up and go pray *Fajr*? Get up lazybones! *Jennah* is way comfier than your bed. So, get up and earn it.

But, things do happen, and you may find yourself in a situation wherein you are absolutely unable to pray, such as driving to the emergency room because your wife is in labor, and the drive is so long you cannot stop for one moment in the entire 4-ish hour window in which prayer is required ... but that isn't realistic. No woman would willingly have to be in a car for four hours in labor, guys. But if, IF such a thing happened, or something similar and slightly more realistic, what then?

Well, then you make up the prayer as soon as possible. Let's say you missed *Fajr* because it's at crazy-o'clock in the morning and you didn't even hear the alarm: pray as soon as you wake up. Get up, make *wudu* (or *ghusl* if need be), and pray. No waiting for coffee or the Facebook/ Twitter/Instagram/Pinterest scroll of death. Wake Up. Make *wudu*. Pray. If it was truly outside of your control, Allah (SWT) is the Most Forgiving.

It's been a crazy day and you get an alert on your phone that *Maghrib* is in 15 minutes and you realize you haven't prayed *Dhuhr* or *Asr*? Pray *Asr* first because you don't want to miss that one too. Then pray *Dhuhr* and *Maghrib* when it is time, etc. There are debates about how to go about this, and we encourage you to go look into those, but generally: pray the prayer required of you in that moment if you are afraid you will miss it, then make up the previous one.

*Salah* is your base operating procedure as a Muslim. If all other deeds are just too much today or tomorrow, you need to still perform your *salah*, all five in their prescribed time. Start incorporating them into your life as best as you can. Make it the focus of your day, the metaphorical hub around which all your other activities orbit. Allow yourself to let the world fade away five times a day and re-center your heart, reconnect with your Lord, and refocus your goals and intentions. If you do that, you are off to a great start!

# 8- Know Thy Sources

Than is the part where we tell you about how you have to do research. But not so much research that you get bored because being bored is the worst. Just joking; it's *shirk*. *Shirk* is the worst.

*'What do you mean, I have to do "research" and can I skip this chapter?'* you may be thinking. Sure, go ahead and skip it. But only if you want to be made into a fool and follow anything as long as it falls from a Muslim's mouth. But if you want to reach Muslim ninja level 9,000[8], then read on.

In Islam, sources are sacred. That's kinda the thing with religions, right? Holy books are sacred. Well, in Islam it goes much deeper than that. Sources in Islam are painstakingly protected and meticulously verified as authentic.

There are two sources of revelation that Muslims believe in. The first is the Quran—which by now we are sure you have at least glanced at. The second source is the *Sunnah*, or the verified practices and commands of Prophet Muhammad (PBUH).

---

[8] There are no "Muslim ninja levels" in case you were concerned as to what level you are at now. Or in case you wanted to know how to get a green belt as a Muslim ninja. It's just for giggles. But go ahead and give yourself 1,000 levels and a baby blue belt when you finish reading this book. You will have earned it!

Prophet Muhammad (PBUH) said, "Read the Quran and act by it. And do not abandon it, do not exceed its limits, do not eat with it [as if it were money], and do not seek more by using it." (Narrated in *al-Jami*)

The word "Quran" means recitation. And that is how the Quran was when it was first revealed to the Prophet (PBUH)—something he recited verbally. It was also written down on whatever the companions of the Prophet could find, namely stones, leather, and bones. There wasn't a ton of paper back in those days (none actually) and our gut tells us that there probably wasn't word processing software either. So, it was not yet in book format.

In addition to being written down on various found objects, it was recited. Often. People listened to it recited in prayer or by the Prophet (PBUH) or by the many people who had it memorized. And there were a lot of those kinds of memorizing people back then. They had to be, what with no paper and all. In fact, theirs was a culture known for being excellent at precise memorization.

The Prophet was sent to an oral community. Most people were not even literate. They really didn't have much need to be. But they could memorize the mess out of something. These people just had a need and developed a knack for it.

The people in the Prophet's (PBUH) time could memorize volumes of information word-for-word. If they were to play a game of "telephone," they would be sure to get every word, and even every inflection, correct. And they would probably be aggravated that we are so terrible at the game.

On top of all of this writing down and

memorizing, the Prophet (PBUH) made sure that everyone had every letter, every sound, every pause pronounced, written, and recited correctly. You will learn how to do all that later when you get to Muslim ninja level 5,000[9].

After the Prophet's death, many of those who had memorized the Quran began dying, as people tend to do. Also, there was a battle where lots of Quran memorizers were killed. A crisis arose, and the leaders of the Muslims had to act quickly to preserve the Quran. The Muslims in charge decided to compile the written pieces of Quran into a book, compare it with those who had it memorized (those who were still alive, of course), and then double and quadruple-check it.

The written (Arabic) version of Quran available to us is literally exactly the same, letter-for-letter, as the one first compiled by those who were among the Prophet (PBUH). Allah (SWT) tells us in the Quran about this preservation: "We have undoubtedly sent down the Reminder, and We will truly preserve it." (Quran 15:9)

The Quran has been preserved. But any translation of the Quran is not considered the Quran itself since it is not in the original language in which it was revealed. A lot is lost in translation. So, we recommend sticking with a few of the more well-known and respected translations. British convert to Islam from the Victorian era named Marmaduke Pickthall translated the Quran too, but he used Victorian English (obviously), so we suggest the newer versions. He did have some pretty awesome stuff to say in the foreword of his translation though. He wrote:

---

[9] See previous footnote.

[...] The Quran cannot be translated [...] The book is here rendered almost literally, and every effort has been made to choose befitting language. But the result is not the Glorious Quran, that inimitable symphony, the very sounds of which move men to tears and ecstasy. It is only an attempt to present the meaning of the Quran and peradventure something of the charm in English. It can never take the place of the Quran in Arabic, nor is it meant to do so [...]. (*The Meanings of the Glorious Qur'an*)

Until you learn to read Arabic and have a sound understanding of Quranic language–which may never happen and that is ok–stick with *Sahih International* or Yusuf Ali's interpretation as they have solid translations for tricky words and great footnotes for verses that have implied meanings and/or are metaphorical. These translations are one of few translations that are not overshadowed by weird cultural interpretations or strange word meanings. But, you gotta understand that while you read these interpretations you are not getting the full weight and meaning of the Quran. That only comes with knowing and understanding Quranic Arabic.

You know how life gets complicated and you just wish you had a manual to make it simpler? Well, this is it. No ... not *this*, as in the *Field Guide*, though we certainly hope you find it helpful, but we mean the Quran. The Quran is your ultimate guide to life. Read it. Follow it. Try to get a deeper and deeper understanding of it. We are still people trying to struggle with our own selves and the world around us. The Quran was revealed to all of us to show us how to live a focused, peaceful, purposeful, contented, and examined life.

"[...] And whoever obeys Allah and His Messenger, Allah shall admit him in the Gardens underneath which rivers flow [...]" (Quran 4:13)

The word *"sunnah"* in Arabic literally means "the path or the way." We know about the *Sunnah* or the way of Prophet Muhammad (PBUH) by reading the *ahadith.* The *ahadith* (collected narrations of the life of the Prophet) were narrated by men and women who were trustworthy and could prove their direct chain of reference to the Prophet. Then scholars collected and verified these men and women's reliability and every link in their chains of narration.

A *hadith* (singular of *ahadith*) is a singular narration about the life of the Prophet Muhammad (PBUH) or what he approved of, as opposed to the entirety of his path or way, which is the *Sunnah.* Since the meaning of the word *"sunnah"* is "path," think about the *Sunnah* like a pathway of stones or bricks; the *hadith* are the individual bricks that make up the path. Each *hadith* is another stepping stone that makes up the *Sunnah,* or the path.

Both the Quran and *Sunnah* are essential; one cannot practice Islam without consulting both of them—as the Quran tells us. The *Sunnah* fills in all the details about how to live our best life, one that is most pleasing to Allah (SWT). It's kinda like you got an instruction manual (the Quran) to life, and Allah, in His infinite wisdom sent a guy with the manual to show us how it's done right. This is the same reason all the Prophets (PBUT) were sent: as an example of how to live and worship in a way that is optimal for our own souls.

The point is that the *Sunnah* is not just a collection

of stories about how some guy lived, it is the example of a life divinely-inspired by Allah (SWT). It is direct revelation from Allah, or decisions of the Messenger (PBUH) that were then confirmed by revelation. The *Sunnah* is a part of the revelation. If Allah (SWT) had willed, He would have only sent a book to guide humankind and not sent it through any messenger. But Allah didn't only send down a book. He sent the Quran to the Prophet Muhammad (PBUH). He informed Prophet Muhammad (and all prophets) of the divine revelation and appointed him to convey it, explain it, and live it as an example to humankind. As a mercy to humankind, Allah sent a book of truth–the Quran–and an example of how to live according to it—The Prophet Muhammad. "Verily, We have revealed the Reminder (Quran to you, Oh Muhammad) so that you may explain to people what has been revealed to them." (Quran 16:64)

## LATER MADE-UP *HADITH* (FABRICATIONS)

But before you go out and believe every *hadith* you hear, know that not all *hadith* are created equal.

Some *hadith* are not even from the Prophet (PBUH) even though some people claim they are. These are called fabricated *hadith*, meaning someone just made it up and said that the Prophet said it. Some *hadith* are weak, meaning that they do not have enough evidence to support the claim that they have come from the Prophet. Some *hadith* are authentic or *sahih*, meaning we can trace the saying, with certainty, back to the messenger himself.

There is a whole rating system of *hadith* so that we do not start building our religion off some fake stuff Joe Shmoe made up and attributed to the Prophet (PBUH). The highest and most authentic *hadith* are known as *sahih*. It's not super important that you know all the terms for the authentic ratings of *hadith* right now. You have enough terminology to remember and a huge learning curve ahead of you already.

Just know that if someone is telling you about a *hadith* and they can't cite a source or that source is not *sahih*, don't trust it. Like ... at all. Later, as you rise in Muslim ninja levels, you will learn more about what makes a *hadith* authentic. The scholars of yore came up with an entire science behind rating *hadith*, chain of narration, and all the painstakingly detailed biographies that went into compiling and verifying authenticity.

Know that yes, bad people exist, and those bad people will sometimes make up stuff about the faith to manipulate people. And sometimes ignorant people will quote *hadith* that do not have any authenticity. When this happens, and you don't do your research by checking sources, bad things can happen. So, ask people to cite their sources. It's not rude. It's smart. And most people will gladly share their sources with you.

There are some collections of *ahadith* that are the most trusted and widely used among Muslims. These are *Ibn Majah, Dawud, Tirmidhi, Muslim,* and *Bukhari,* the last two being the most trustworthy of the most trustworthy. These are the names of some scholars who compiled collections of the most authentic *ahadith*. So, these are their names and also the name of their collections.

When you see one of these names in parentheses after the words "Narrated in," e.g.: (Narrated in *Bukhari*), after a *hadith* has been quoted, you know it's to cite the source of the *hadith* and to show you that it is authentic and can be trusted as having actually

94

come from the mouth or life of Prophet Muhammad (PBUH).

Authenticity is why you will see these names in parentheses throughout this book. We are citing our *hadith* sources from the most authentic sources for your learning pleasure. You might have been thinking that up 'til now we just like throwing extra words at the end of quotes for fun, and we do, but that is not the only reason.

So, the Quran and the *Sunnah* are what we base our religion on. If anyone tells you to do something because it is a part of Islam, ask them where they got it from. If it's not from one of these two sources, it is most likely from their culture and it is not a part of Islam. This is not to say that everything from different cultures is bad, but that people should not push a cultural directive on others and falsely call it an Islamic directive. And this is also not to say that just because it has an authentic source in the Quran or *Sunnah* that those quoting it to you aren't quoting it out of context or from a bad translation.

ISLAM IS NOT A DO IT YOURSELF RELIGION

Now that we have told you all about going to the sources of Islamic knowledge to verify what people tell you, this doesn't mean that Islam is DIY. You can't just go and read the Quran and *Sunnah* and think you can understand everything about Islam and make *fatawa* (rulings) for yourself. You *should* read these sources, but you should also find a scholar whom you trust to learn from and can help you understand the full textual and historical context of the Quran and *Sunnah*, the *Sahabah*'s (companions of the Prophet— apostles) and the classical scholars' interpretations of rulings, and how all of this applies in your time and place.

That's a lot of stuff, right? That's the point. There is an entire body of knowledge that surrounds one *hadith* or one verse of the Quran that can have different implications for you today than it did back in the 7th or the 10th or even the 18th century. There are *ahadith* that balance each other out and verses that qualify each other and verses that qualify *hadith* and so on. And there are certain circumstances that have to be in play for a Quranic or Prophetic directive to be applicable. And one needs an understanding of cultural appropriateness back in the 7th century and how that translates to us today.

And then there is an entire world of linguistic knowledge that is fundamental to all this understanding. This is why people spend their whole lives learning classical Arabic to study just one discipline of Islamic knowledge and still only think of themselves as students of knowledge. Allah (SWT) says in the Quran: "Say, 'If the sea were ink for [writing] the words of my Lord, the sea would be exhausted before the words of my Lord were exhausted, even if We brought the like of it as a supplement.'" (Quran 18:109)

Knowledge is vast, and we must have reverence for that. We cannot go off half-cocked and think we can sew together a few *ahadith* here and a few *ayat* there without any background or context or even an understanding of the source text language *and voila!* have a picture of what Islam is all about. We need scholars.

This might sound contradictory to the advice to know your sources. But in reality, it is only the Islamic way of taking the middle path. Do not place your *deen* in someone else's hands (other than the prophets) and follow them blindly. For sure, if you do

96

that, your heart will be broken. You should look for proof from people and only trust Allah (SWT) with that kind of ultimate trust. But we should also look to the scholars for a more complete picture of our religion. They know some stuff. Do we have to trust everything they say? No. Should we stop listening to them if we disagree with one or two of their opinions? No. People are flawed and for that reason we should balance this equation. Trust in Allah (SWT), but tie your camel, as the Muslims say.

## SCHOLARS WE RECOMMEND

Below is a list of some of the scholars we believe are trustworthy and understand the modern, Western cultural context and the convert experience. Some of them are converts themselves. You can feel free to listen to any scholar you want, but know that if they say something that sounds seriously messed-up, it probably is. So, check the sources. All of these scholars have a strong online presence. Googling them will lead you to their knowledge. So, Google away!

- Suhaib Webb
- Mufti Menk
- Dr. Shabir Ally
- Anse Tamara Gray
- Omar Suleiman
- Yasir Qadhi
- Ingrid Mattson
- Yasmin Mogahed (she is not technically a scholar, but girl got some serious wisdom)
- Siraj Wahhaj
- Hamza Yusuf

This is usually the part where I talk about my experiences with the situation mentioned in the chapter. I have many in this case. But I thought it might be more fun for us to take a look at some made up (or fabricated) *hadith* and make fun of them.

Again, all of these *ahadith* I am quoting were never said by the Prophet (PBUH). They were made up by people who wanted to manipulate the religion to suit their own desires. I would NEVER EVER make fun of any authentic *hadith*, and neither should you. That is dangerous territory.

But since these are all from unscrupulous liars, game on!

Made up *hadith*:
Love the Arabs for three reasons: because I, Muhammad (PBUH) am an Arab, the Holy Quran was revealed in Arabic, and the language of *Jennah* will be Arabic. (Classified as false by Al-Haakim)

Theresa's Response: Never happened, but nice try. We know from a very authentic *hadith* that the Prophet (PBUH) actually said, "All mankind is from Adam and Eve, an Arab has no superiority over a non-Arab nor a non-Arab has any superiority over an Arab; also, a white has no superiority over a black, nor a black has any superiority over a white—except by piety and good action. Learn that every Muslim is a brother to every Muslim and that the Muslims constitute one brotherhood." This *hadith* is quoted in all the authentic biographies of the Prophet including *Al Seerah Annabawiyah* by Ibn Hisham.

Made up *hadith*:
Prayer performed in a turban is equivalent to 15

prayers without a turban. And a *Jumuah* prayer performed in a turban is equivalent to 10 *Jumuah* prayers without a turban. Verily, the angels wear turbans for the *Jumuah* prayer and they continue to send blessings on the people who wear turbans until sunset. (Classified as fabricated by Ibn Hajar)

Theresa's response: Does someone have a turban fetish? Like what is the deal? Seriously!?

Made up *hadith*:
If it weren't for women, Allah would have been worshipped properly. (Related by Ibn Adee–a man in the chain of narration has been deemed a liar)

Theresa's Response: Allah (SWT) is worshipped properly by Muslims, including women, who follow the Quran and *Sunnah*. Mary (PBUH) the mother of Isa (PBUH) has a whole chapter in the Quran named after her because of how perfectly she worshipped Allah. Whoever made this malarkey up was an angry and ignorant misogynist.

## CANDID KAIGHLA

Like so many new converts, I made the terrible mistake of getting married 2.5 seconds after I converted to Islam (ok, not really ... more like 2.5 months). But, one of the reasons I jumped at the chance and chose that particular dude was that he was a *sheikh* or *imam* (preacher).

I, sweet naive little convert that I was, imagined that if I married a *sheikh* like him–someone with two master's degrees in *ahadith* and *fiqh* (that's Arabic for all the rules in Islam ever)–he would really be a super good Muslim and would teach me tons, and it would

99

all be correct, 'cuz it was coming from the horse's mouth, as it were.

Big mistake. Massive mistake for a hundred reasons, but the main reason is this: anything and everything that came out of his mouth I took to be Gospel truth (pun intended). If he told me $x$ was *haram*, I stopped it immediately and told all my friends to stop it, too. If he told me $y$ was required and people who don't do it are bad Muslims, I believed him and judged people (and myself) accordingly.

It took six years and a thousand terrible experiences, but I soon came to see that he, like some other religious leaders of all religions, was teaching me his culture, not the pure religion. Had I ever asked him for a source, I may have learned that he was intentionally deluding me. But, I trusted him because of his position, and he used that to his advantage.

We cannot allow our understanding of the religion to be based on weak (sometimes authentic but taken out of context) or even totally made-up stories about our prophets (PBUT). It's not hard to see how this can create a domino effect in the community so that as long as person $x$ says something, person $y$ believes it and shares it with persons $a$, $b$, and $c$. And the lie perpetuates.

# 9-Slow and Steady

We understand that what makes converts so, so zealous from Day One is the same quality that made them consider Islam in the first place. It's the same quality that will keep them going in the long-haul. And that is their devotion to truth.

We understand how you feel. Islam has cost you something, even if it was only drinking with your buddies or having a boyfriend. For many of us, though, it's far greater a price we pay to embrace this religion. Many of us lose our closest friends, our dearest family members, and some are kicked out of their homes and fired from their jobs. The truth is expensive. Why would anyone pay such a high price to accept and practice a religion and then not give it their all?

So, we tell ourselves that the day after our *shahada*, we will be praying all five prayers right on the dot, plus the extra *Sunnah* prayers, wearing full *niqab* and *abaya* or *thobe* and a lumberjack beard, fasting every Monday and Thursday, and trying to memorize the entire Quran in a year.

While this devotion is respectable and impressive, it's both unlikely to continue and highly dangerous to the overall *iman* of a new Muslim to imagine they can incorporate so many new habits overnight. The worst thing that can come from this is total burnout and a feeling that Islam is *just. too. hard.* The Messenger of Allah (PBUH) said:

> The *deen* [religion] is ease. Whoever makes the *deen* too hard for himself will be overpowered, so direct yourselves to what is right, follow a middle course, accept the good news of the reward for right action, and seek help [to reach your goal by being constant in worshipping] in the morning, evening, and some of the night. (Narrated in *Bukhari*)

He also said, "take up good deeds [in addition to the obligatory pillars] only as much as you are able, for the best deeds are those done regularly even if they are few." (Narrated in *Ibn Majah*) When Islam feels like it's too difficult, and when it feels like you can't breathe, this is your first sign that it's not really Islam you're trying to follow.

### THE PROPHET (PBUH) HIMSELF WAS BALANCED

If anyone on this earth had a right to say what's important as a Muslim and what's not, it's Prophet Muhammad (PBUH). Surely, if Allah (SWT) had wanted us to do everything in one go, and spend all our days and nights in worship, He would have commanded Prophet Muhammad to do that, and to teach us as much. But that's not what happened. The Messenger of Allah (PBUH) said to one of his companions:

> 'Oh Abdullah, I am told you fast all day and pray all night.' I said, 'Of course, O Messenger of Allah.' The Prophet said: 'Do not do so. Fast and break your fast, pray in the night and sleep. Verily, your body has a right over you, your eyes have a right over you, and your wife has a right over you'. (Narrated in *Bukhari*)

102

Many people don't understand that fulfilling the rights of one's body, spouse, family, etc. are also acts of worship because they too bring us closer to Allah (SWT), and so they too deserve our attention. Prayer has its place, fasting has its place; these are great things to establish and do extra of when we can. But if they are getting in the way of taking care of business, so to speak, these kinds of worship are no longer a good thing. Putting things in their place and understanding balance is the secret to success.

## LESSON FROM THE COMPANIONS OF PROPHET MUHAMMAD (PBUH)

Islam wasn't revealed in a day and you are not expected to learn it or adhere to it in a day. Please know with certainty that all that is required of you to be a Muslim is to do your best to surrender to God. The last thing we want is for you to feel overwhelmed with too much, too quickly and decide to just give up. The name of the game in Islam is balance, moderation, and keeping to the middle path.

To illustrate this fact, we can look to the repeal of alcohol and other intoxicants in the early years of Islamic history. In general, anything which intoxicates a person to the point that they are not thinking clearly is *haram*. That means alcohol, over-the-counter drugs used in excess, street drugs, peyote, and other such "natural" drugs, and the like. But these intoxicants were not always *haram*. In fact, for 13+ years after the first revelation, Allah (SWT) was completely silent on the issue of drinking alcohol and ingesting intoxicants. More than 13 years. Let that soak in for a minute.

During his lifetime, Prophet Muhammad (PBUH) would have been surrounded by people who drank

103

and even became drunk. The people of his society made alcoholic drinks from things like grapes, dates, wheat, barley, and even honey. Had Allah wanted to, He could have declared alcohol *haram* from the get-go, but He, in in His infinite wisdom, saw that this would overburden the new Muslims.

It wasn't until around the third or fourth year after the *hijrah* (or migration of the Muslims to Madinah) that Allah (SWT) made being drunk during *salah haram*: "O you who have believed, do not approach prayer while you are intoxicated until you know what you are saying [...]." (Quran 4:43)

Then, it wasn't until six or seven years after the *hijrah* that Allah revealed in *Surah al-Ma'idah* (the fifth *surah*, or chapter, of the Quran) that drinking alcohol, period, was *haram*:

> O you who have believed, indeed, intoxicants, gambling, [sacrificing on] stone altars [to other than Allah], and divining arrows are but defilement from the work of *Shaytan* [Satan], so avoid it that you may be successful. *Shaytan* only wants to cause between you animosity and hatred through intoxicants and gambling and to avert you from the remembrance of Allah and from prayer. So, will you not desist? (Quran 5:90-91)

The first Muslims on the planet didn't even concern themselves with stopping their addiction to alcohol for 13+ years, but it's one of the main things we think about these days when we think about living as a Muslim in the West.

Are we telling you it's cool if you keep drinking? No, of course not. Alcohol is definitely *haram* for us, as spelled out in that last verse we cited. But what we are saying is: everything in Islam, building good habits and getting rid of bad habits, has to be incorporated little-by-little. Otherwise it will not become a habit (or a habit kicked).

If you are an addict of any kind, you must start kicking that habit. But you can take small steps because that is most likely to lead to success. If you are in a *haram* relationship, take the steps to end that relationship, even if they are small steps. If you are having a hard time praying five times a day, take smaller steps to build that habit.

As long as you are doing your best to move away from *haram*, you are moving in the right direction. As long as you are doing your best to move toward the *halal* and the obligatory, you are on the right track. If you feel yourself overwhelmed, keep up your baseline prayer for the health of your faith, but take a break from the extra. If you feel as if you are getting the hang of things, try to incorporate a little more. Building good habits and getting rid of bad ones takes time. So, do not feel defeated if it doesn't magically happen overnight. And do not push yourself too hard.

## THE HARAM-LOADER

Your heritage Muslim friends know it's their duty to help you. They don't want you to fall prey to weird sects or extreme beliefs out there. Neither do we. They also want to make sure you are getting what you need in terms of faith and life. Same here. But many of these good-hearted, concerned *ummah* citizens often try to help the new Muslims by drowning them in a list of do's and don'ts, *halal* and *haram*. They see you as a fully-grown adult, an eager new Muslim who simply needs your cup filled with knowledge, someone who should be doing everything he/she can to be Muslims like them.

105

What these heritage Muslim probably do not even realize is that everything they know about Islam was gathered over a lifetime of learning, of seeing people do and abstain. They didn't come out of their mother knowing when *Fajr* is. They also didn't know, at the age of 12, that fasting gets easier the more you do it. Even the convert who's been around a while might have forgotten how many years it took to get where he/she is today. But you, as a brand-new Muslim, are just like a brand-new baby in all ways Islamic. And as such you are not ready to be loaded down with all that is *haram* and *halal*. It is overwhelming. Take a moment to read the following definition (we made up) and ask yourself if you know or have ever met a heritage Muslim or long time convert that fits this description: Haram-Loader (n.)- a person who dumps a bunch of opinions of what is *haram* onto the new Muslim's already-full plate.

As a new Muslim, you have a ton of other stuff to deal with already: *How will I tell my family? ... How will I be able to learn how to say the prayers in a strange and difficult language? ... How will I make new Muslim friends? ... Why do people make it so damn awkward at the masjid?* It goes on and on. You have a lot on your mind, and sometimes your fellow Muslims, instead of facilitating this transition as they should, unwittingly end up putting more on your plate. But haram-loading can extinguish new, budding faith faster than blowing out a candle. So, what are you to do if, or when, you encounter such a person/situation?

FOLLOW THESE 5 SIMPLE STEPS
WHEN YOU ENCOUNTER A HARAM-LOADER

1- Remember that Islam is not a list of *haram* and *halal*. This is dangerous reductionism that needs to be avoided at all costs. You will learn all that you need to know. And you will be excited to incorporate it into your life when and as you can if the foundation of your faith (understanding who Allah is and learning the pillars) is strong.

2- Be patient when people try to tell you everything in your life is *haram*. They just want to help. And sometimes heritage Muslims are using the term "*haram*" as an idiom that does not literally mean *haram*. And sometimes things they think are *haram* are simply their opinion.

3- You are more vulnerable than heritage Muslims and sometimes that means what is *haram* for someone else might not be *haram* for you. Sometimes heritage Muslims forget or don't know this. Make sure you have a plan before you go off quitting your job, or selling your home, or doing anything that will jeopardize you feeding yourself and your children, keeping clothes on your back, and a roof over your head just because someone told you that something is *haram*. You are not surrounded by a Muslim family or support system to make sure you are cared or provided for. Slow your roll before you leap.

4- Learn the pillars of Islam and *iman* in depth. We have provided a chapter for each in this book that do not even scratch the surface of really, truly understanding these pillars. These are the basis of your faith in practice and belief. You can learn all the other details that do not deal with these pillars in due time. If someone tries to talk to you about all that is *haram*, kindly ask them to explain to you more about the pillars.

5- If someone tries to talk to you about all that is *haram*, and they have finished telling you all they know about the pillars, then kindly ask them to tell you more about Allah (SWT) Learn the names and attributes of Allah and how they impact you. Nothing will strengthen your heart and give you peace more than understanding all that you can about who Allah is. When you know Allah (SWT), everything falls into place. A good resource for learning about your Lord is the book *A Temporary Gift: Reflections on Love, Loss, and Healing* by Asmaa Hussein. It is one woman's journey through grief and healing after the murder of her husband. But it is also a story of coming nearer to Allah (SWT) by understanding His names and attributes and His mercy and knowledge. It is extremely well-written and touching. And through Asmaa's journey, the reader cannot help but also come closer to Allah and better understand who Allah is.

# 10- *What the Hijab?!:*
# *Men & Women*

We are not going to go through and explain each and every Islamic law regarding *hijab* because, well, we don't have the qualifications, the patience, or the space in this book for that. And also, because we trust that you have the spiritual maturity to open your heart up to guidance from Allah (SWT) beyond the *shahada*. This is your path: learning, finding where to draw the line in the sand, figuring out what is more than you can handle, and loving what makes your heart shine. This is your journey to Allah.

However, this one little command about *hijab* from Allah (SWT) has been talked about, measured, found to be too much, and not enough all at the same time. So, we thought we would attempt to untangle the mess of perceptions that surround such a simple thing as modesty.

## WHAT IS *HIJAB?*

What most people call *hijab* is really just the headscarf worn by Muslim women. So, saying *"hijab"* when you mean something that covers the hair is inaccurate. *Hijab* is more than just a hair covering; it's a basic standard of modesty given to humankind from our Creator (SWT). So, what is this basic standard? Well, it depends on who you are.

Yes, *hijab* is for men too. It's often forgotten since many people, men and women, spend so much time telling women what they should and shouldn't wear that they forget about how men are also supposed to observe modesty. The fact is that God commanded men to be modest in their dress *before* He commanded the same thing of women:

> Tell the believing men to reduce [some] of their vision and guard their private parts. That is purer for them. Indeed, Allah is acquainted with what they do. And tell the believing women to reduce [some] of their vision and guard their private parts and not expose their adornment except that which [necessarily] appears thereof and to wrap [a portion of] their head-covers over their chests and not expose their adornment [...] (Quran 24:30-31)

Modesty, as it is defined for men, primarily means controlling their eyes, or "lowering their gaze" as many translations say. That means, in modern terms, check your male gaze at the door-don't go around checking out every female that comes in your path. In fact, don't check out *any* of them, except the one you are married to. It's immodest, it's disrespectful, and it's just bad manners.

But beyond refraining from ogling women, there is also a standard of dress for men that directs men to cover everything from above the navel (belly button) to below the knees with opaque, loose clothing. This is the minimum you must cover, but more is better. Seriously, don't go around without a shirt on just because you can. It's weird. And skinny jeans? Nope. Part of modesty for men includes loose clothing, and that means wearing pants that don't define or describe your body. Come on, guys. The main idea behind *hijab* for men is obscuring the shape of your body.

*Hijab* for men also means growing out the beard (defined as the hair that grows on the jawline—you can shave the hair that grows on the cheek). The Prophet (PBUH) said, "Keep the beards and cut the mustaches short." (Narrated in *Bukhari*)

### FOR WOMEN

Modesty, or observing *hijab* as it is defined for women, also includes "lowering the gaze." That means exactly what it means for men: don't go around checking out every guy that comes in your path. In fact, don't check out *any* of them, except the one you are married to. It's immodest, it's disrespectful, and it's just bad manners. According to the majority of Sunni scholars, the *hijab* for sisters is also a standard of dress that covers everything except the hands, feet, and face with opaque, loose clothing, in whatever way you choose to incorporate that into your cultural and personal identity.[10]

So, what does all this mean for you? Well, it means two things: 1.) yes, *hijab* is an Islamic requirement 2.) it doesn't mean that if you choose not to follow this requirement you are any less Muslim than the next brother or sister. As you may have noticed, *hijab* was not once mentioned in the five pillars of Islam or the six pillars of *iman*. So, it is not a basis of faith or a

---

[10] There are too many rulings to cite here about what *hijab* means for women and what is meant to be covered. We encourage you to find out more. A great resource to do so is beliefnet.com.

defining aspect of one's Islam. As a new Muslim, after learning the basic pillars, you need to take on Islamic requirements at your own pace. If wearing *hijab* right out the gate is too much—and it is for a lot of sisters for whom *hijab* will change their day-to-day lives—then know that you must walk before you can run and doing things at your pace is perfectly fine. Allah (SWT) knows your situation, intentions, what you can handle, and what you cannot. Do what you can, when you can.

However, dear sisters, we are sad to report from the field that the people you meet *will* judge you and your level of faith based on what you wear or don't wear, no matter what, because people are superficial and like to control women by controlling (or trying to control) their appearance. Whether it is a Muslim finding fault with the length of your skirt or a non-Muslim arrogantly pretending to "know" you are oppressed because of the scarf on your head, we sisters are getting pummeled from all directions no matter what we do. The fact is, even if we weren't Muslims, all women experience some form of this "damned if you do, damned if you don't" treatment. But it is more intensified for Muslim women because so much meaning is put into *hijab*, and more meaning than is actually there. If you don't observe *hijab,* your faith-based community will likely treat you as somehow "less Muslim." And if you do observe *hijab,* your non-Muslim community will treat you like you have lost your mind.

So, be the boss lady you are and do whatever it is that you need to do. Haters will indeed hate. But do NOT ever even think about observing *hijab*—or not—because you think it will make people happy with you. First of all, if you are observing *hijab* out of peer pressure, you are wasting your time. Your intentions are what matter to Allah (SWT). If you're observing *hijab* to please anyone other than Allah, your time, efforts, and what *hijab* may cost you are wasted.

But, if you are not observing *hijab*–or you are–do not let it be because you are afraid of what people will think. You will NEVER be able to please people. Never, full stop. At least you have a chance of pleasing Allah (SWT), and people cannot reward you as Allah can. So basically, pleasing people is an insanity-inducing endeavor. Never forget you are on your own path, and if it leads you to places no one you know has ever been and those around you won't follow, that's OK because your path is heading toward Allah.

### TALES FROM THERESA TOWN

Before I accepted Islam, I had fever dreams about *hijab*. *Hijab*—or covering my hair as I thought the term meant—was just another road block on the way to becoming Muslim. Was I superficial? Yup! You better believe it. But also, I was young and had little spiritual maturity. I knew I loved Islam. It made sense to me—worship the One who made everything and follow the messengers He sent for guidance to universal truth. Simple. Logical. What's not to love?

But I thought that being Muslim meant that I would have to swaddle myself in hideously un-creative clothing. Visions of black trash bag-esque dresses danced through my nightmares. Now, there is nothing wrong with dressing in monochromatic tones if that's your thing. But it is not mine. I love color and fashion.

Giving up my sense of style wasn't my only concern. I also feared what people would think. I let this get between me and my deep desire to accept

113

Allah's (SWT) guidance. I let it get in my way for some time. But my desire to come closer to Allah mounted. I couldn't *not* be Muslim anymore. I tried to fit into what society expected of me, but I grew increasingly angry and it was breaking me. I couldn't *not* be who I was created to be. So, in desperation, I told my only Muslim friend how I felt about Islam and how I felt about *hijab*.

That friend said something that changed my life. She said: observing *hijab* doesn't make someone Muslim, and not observing it certainly doesn't make someone a non-Muslim. You can become a Muslim now and then think about *hijab* as you learn more. Who knows? You may never wear *hijab*, but at least you have a chance to live and die as a Muslim. And who knows? You might end up wearing it and loving it.

I said my *shahada* shortly after listening to my friend's advice. My plan was to never wear *hijab*, ever. But something weird happened as my faith skyrocketed. I stopped caring about what others thought. I just couldn't give a crap. I was in love with Allah (SWT) and didn't care who knew it. So, two months after I declared myself to be a Muslim, I started observing *hijab* in increments, beginning with the headscarf and then more loose clothing as I grew as a Muslim.

I learned that I didn't have to give up my identity to be modest. I discovered that modesty doesn't necessitate being frumpy. And observing *hijab* has some major perks, one of which is that I don't have to obsess over my coif.

If you consider the fact that before Islam I would spend at least five hours a week grooming my mane, and since observing *hijab*, I maybe spend only one hour a week on my hair. I have so much more time to do other fun things, like write this book. Yay!

# 11- The Masjid: What to Know Before You Go

Going to the *masjid* can be a scary endeavor when you are a new Muslim. Really, going anywhere where you are new can be a scary thing. But going to a place of worship when you are not quite sure what is taboo and what is deemed appropriate behavior is on a whole other level of intimidating. The good news is there is only one first trip; all the next visits will be no big deal. So, rip off that Band-Aid with our guide to making the first trip to the *masjid* as smooth as possible.

A *masjid* is quite different from other places of worship in other faith traditions. The *masjid* is not your fancy temple or mega church complex. The first thing that you might notice upon entering a *masjid* is that there are very few chairs. This does not mean that we are all supposed to stand around the whole time. Sitting on the floor is the norm in the *masjid*. And where there are chairs, they are reserved for the old, pregnant, and infirm. So, unless you are in one of these categories, it would be weird if you popped a squat in one of the few chairs available. Though we Westerners are not used to sitting on the floor, for people in the rest of the world, it's normal.

It's not like *masajid* (plural for *masjid*) can't afford to buy chairs; sitting on the floor is a way of leveling statuses that are all too important outside the *masjid*. Likewise, we line up to pray in no particular order, race, class, or any other classification. The king and the pauper must stand side-by-side in prayer and sit side-by-side on the floor when not in prayer. The only distinction between people is by level of faith and only Allah (SWT) truly knows that. So, have a seat and stay awhile.

Shoes are not allowed on the floor of the prayer area since we walk over all kinds of nasty things on the ground on a day-to-day basis, building up all kinds of bacteria and what-not on the soles of our shoes. When we pray, we need a clean place in which to do so, most especially because of the fact that we literally put our faces on the floor in prayer. To try to keep the floor clean, shoes gotta stay behind.

Usually, you will need to take off your shoes either before you enter or as soon as you have entered the *masjid*. You will know when to take off your shoes because there is usually a shoe shelf, a sign saying take off your shoes, and/or a huge pile of shoes, smells included.

But what about the rest of your outfit? The key to dressing when going to the *masjid* is modesty. Both men and women should dress modestly when visiting the local *masjid*. This means no skinny jeans and tank tops, boys and girls. Modesty is a highly-valued virtue in Islam, both in character and dress. Wear long, loose, opaque clothing, and if you are a lady and happen to own a scarf, it can't hurt to cover your hair (some of you may already be doing all this on the reg.—props to you). Some *masajid* have rules stating women must wear *hijab* in the *masjid*. And if you intend to pray, ya gotta cover your hair.

THE OPPOSITE SEX AT THE *MASJID*

Going in through the wrong entrance at the *masjid* may create a sticky situation. But why are there different entrances, you ask? Well, most *masajid* have separate prayer areas for men and women, and separate entrances for each area. This segregation of the areas was not the practice of the Prophet (PBUH), but people seem to think it was. To be clear, the lines of prayer were separated by sex during the Prophet's time so that worshippers would not to be distracted by libido during worship, but men and women prayed in the same room.[11]

This new-fangled way of separating prayer rooms by sex comes from cultural interpretation and traditional mores in different parts of the world. It's a big thing because women's areas are usually not as spacious or nice as men's areas. Separate is rarely, if ever, equal.

But don't worry! We sisters are out there working for change in this and all matters that are decidedly un-Islamic. Here's to hoping you are reading this at some point in the future and this issue has been rectified in every *masjid* around the world and that we are all travelling around on actual hovering hoverboards that we were promised in the 1980s. If so, yay!

Back to the matter at hand, walking into the wrong area at the *masjid* is like walking into the wrong restroom in a public place. People get really sensitive about it *rolls eyes*. Usually there are signs, or someone will tell you which entrance is which. But if you do end up walking into a room (once you have taken your shoes off) full of people of the opposite sex, just casually tell them you need to find the

---

[11] Kutty, Shaikh Ahmad. *askthescholar.com.*

women's/men's entrance because you are new there. They will understand, *inshaAllah*.

Walking into the wrong room is one thing and usually not a big deal if you explain yourself. But touching someone of the opposite sex is a huge no-no. You might have already learned or ascertained from the *masjid* separation of the sexes that Muslims have strict inter-sex guidelines. When you meet someone of the opposite sex at the *masjid* (or anywhere), don't offer to shake their hand or try to give them a big ole hug.

As a Muslim, you should only be touching people of the opposite sex to whom you are married or those who are members of your immediate family. Not getting touchy-feely with the opposite sex is an excellent way of cutting off, at the root, more inappropriate touching from happening. Some Muslims are a little laxer and will shake hands, but it is considered especially weird to do at our place of worship.

Feel free to shake hands or even hug people of the same sex as you. European-style cheek kissing is very popular at the *masjid*. But this too can be tricky. Which cheek does it start on? How many kisses? Two? Three? Four?! There are as many cheek-kissing styles as there are people. Just make sure you turn your face, or you may get one planted on the lips!

MASJID MANNERS

And while we're on the subject of lips, most of the rest of the general *masjid* manners have something to do with the mouth. Whether it is talking loudly, or eating, there are good manners to be followed when at the *masjid*, but also in your daily life in general.

Manners are very important. Prophet Muhammad

119

(PBUH) said, "And what is most likely to send people to Paradise? Being conscious of Allah and good manners." (Narrated in *Bukhari*)

First things first, don't be loud or curse. This is just common courtesy. Yelling and cursing is usually looked down on in general, unless you are at a sporting event, in a fist fight, or at a bar. Feel free to talk (except when people are actually praying or giving a lecture), but keep it polite. In today's world, cursing is so ubiquitous that it might be hard to check yourself if you have a predilection for profanity (we can relate). But just give it your best attempt. All you can do is try and apologize if you slip up.

The next on the list of mouthy manners involves food. Lots of eating happens at the *masjid*. Yay! Food! So, it's important to know a thing or two about eating etiquette before going to the *masjid* or, again, for general life purposes. The first thing that you need to know is that a Muslim uses his or her right hand to eat. The right hand is used for all things clean and the left hand is used to clean oneself ... like, in the bathroom, we mean. The Prophet (PBUH) said: "If one of you eats, he should eat with his right hand. And if he drinks something, he should drink with his right hand. For indeed, *Shaytan* eats and drinks with his left hand." (Narrated in *Muslim*)

So, eating with the hand you clean yourself with is a bit unsavory, to say the least. Sure, we all have tons of antibacterial gels, foaming soaps, and hand-sanitizers, but germs are invisible to the naked eye and you never know what is still on your hand. Save yourself from intestinal distress. Follow the advice of the Prophet (PBUH). Be different from the *Shaytan*, and eat with your clean hand, even if you are a lefty like Theresa.

The second thing you should keep in mind when

120

enjoying exotic dishes at the *masjid*, and in general, is to say, "*Bismillah*" (in the name of Allah) before you eat. You don't need to say it out loud, but you should at least mouth it out. The Prophet (PBUH) explained (and we are paraphrasing) that *Shaytan* partakes in the food if the name of Allah (SWT) is not recited at the start of eating. However, if one forgets to say "*Bismillah*" at the beginning of partaking in the food, and then remembers and says it, *Shaytan* is made to vomit what he has eaten. (Narrated in *Muslim*) It's kind of like don't feed the gremlins, right? Don't feed the *Shaytan*. Say "*Bismillah*" so they cannot partake in your meal.

If you are kind enough to bring food to the *masjid* to share with all, make sure you are not bringing something that is *haram*. In Western countries, pork (esp. gelatin) and alcohol products are snuck into many different products. So, be sure to read the food labels of your ingredients before you share.

**Disclaimer:** brothers, please do continue reading, despite our bold heading that this section is "For the Ladies," because you might need to know this info for future/current wife and/or daughter(s).

Some people will tell you that you cannot go to the *masjid* when you are on your period. Some people say you can go, as long as you don't walk in the prayer area. Some people say you can go and dance around the place, no problem (not literally dance, but you get it).

The truth is that we (Kaighla and Theresa, specifically) don't know. All we know is that everyone has a different opinion and it is probably best that you respect the opinion of your local *masjid* board. If you live in an area with many *masajid* and many different opinions, and you are a lady on your period who wants to go to the *masjid*, then find one that is cool with that.

The only thing we know for sure on this topic is that ladies put prayer (and we mean *salah*) on hold during menstruation.[12] *Dua* and other forms of worship are encouraged during this time of the month to maintain your connection with Allah (SWT). But it is a time when you get a *salah* hall pass.

Now that you know the general rules of the road, you should also know that you don't need a *masjid* to pray. Prophet Muhammad (PBUH) said, "The earth has been made for me [and for my *ummah*] as a *masjid* and a pureness; therefore, anyone of my *ummah* can pray whenever the time of prayer is due." (Narrated in *Bukhari*)

As the *hadith* says, Allah (SWT) has made the entire earth a place of prayer and we can pop out a few units of prayer when the time comes wherever we are, as long as that place is clean, (reads: don't pray in the bathroom). But you should still go to the *masjid* at some point. It is important to have community around you to support you on your journey and to help guide you in the right direction.

TALES FROM THERESA TOWN

I, Theresa Corbin, am a repeat perpetrator of *masjid* faux pas. My first faux pas was once refusing to take my shoes off because the shoes I was wearing made my feet smelly. I know that is gross, but they were such cute shoes! So, I thought it would be less offensive to keep my shoes on.

---

[12] *Sahih al-Bukhari.* "Book of Menstrual Periods."

It was not. Everyone mean-mugged me the whole time and refused to talk to me (this actually happened in a *musallah*—a designated prayer area—and not the *masjid* proper, but still). If your feet are smelly, take your shoes off and ask to be directed to the restroom where you can wash off the funk. I promise people are constantly washing their feet at the masjid. It's a part of *wudu*.

My second faux pas was when I was a newbie and less-aware of Muslim manners. I would attend prayer in tight shirts. No one said anything, but all that staring makes sense now that I get the concept of modesty and that long sleeves don't make something modest if it is skin tight. But it was a norm for me to wear tight clothing, so I didn't think anything of it because my skin was covered.

The third faux pas was actually not **my** faux pas for once. Once upon a time, my husband was a teenager. It is hard to believe, but I've seen the pictures. Now there is nothing wrong with being a teenager, but there is something wrong with being a teenager in the 90s with a piercing and a cross earring, and going to the *masjid* as such. He didn't know any better, but it was pretty funny when he was schooled by a 10-year old.

Faux pas number four: I'm a lefty, which means I do most things with my left hand. Shocking stuff, I know. And prior to Islam I ate with my left hand. But I had heard that Muslims eat with their hands. I was game and wanted to dive into my plate of food using the built-in utensils of my hands, showing that I was savvy. I thought I was so cool. Everyone was questioning me about how I knew to eat with my hands. They smiled a knowing smile but didn't say a peep that I was eating with the wrong hand, a hand that is considered gross to eat with. That's what I get for trying to show off.

Even though I have made a fool out of myself many times at the *masjid* and more times than I am willing to admit outside the *masjid*, I regret nothing! Making mistakes is a part of the process of learning. I will never apologize for trying, fumbling, and learning.

# 12- The Company You Keep

**M**any misguided Muslims will quote the Quranic verse 5:51 when you talk about your non-Muslim friends:
O you who believe! Do not take the Jews and the Christians for friends [*Awliya*]; they are friends of each other; and whoever amongst you takes them for a friend, then surely he is one of them; surely Allah does not guide the unjust people. (Quran 5:51)

This verse may prick up your ears or emotions and sound kind of strange. After all, wouldn't Allah (SWT) want us to befriend and be kind to as many people of all kinds of faiths? Of course! But, let's make the closed-minded Muslims' mindset into a teachable moment, shall we?

When thinking about any verse of the Quran (or *hadith* for that matter), it is super important to understand the historical context and language of the original Arabic. In this verse, the word *"Awliya"* (plural) or *"wali"* (singular) has been (badly) translated as "friends" or "friend."

However, the more appropriate translation would be a "guardian, protector, or advocate." Muslims are to be advocates and protectors for each other, and friends with everyone. Prophet Muhammad (PBUH) was kind to the pagans of Mecca and fought them only when they fought him. He made treaties with the Jews of Madinah and honored the treaties until they broke them. He received the Christians of *Najran* with kindness in Madinah. People of all varieties argued with the Prophet (PBUH) about Islam, but he treated them with honor and respect.

So, what does all this translation and context of the Quran mean? Well, it means that you should be kind and generous to the people in your life and cutting off ties of friendship just because you've converted to Islam is extreme and unnecessary. That being said, if your friends encourage you to do things that are against your newfound faith that you have or are still trying to get away from—things like drinking, doing drugs, clubbing, Netflix-and-chilling, etc.—it might be a good idea to put some distance between you and your friends until they can respect your life choices and not recommend that you go against your faith. A true friend would support you in what you deem best for your life. If your friends aren't doing that once you come to Islam, you have to really examine if they were ever really your friends or just good time, fair-weather pals.

CHOOSING NEW FRIENDS

*New Friends? Why do I need new friends just because I am now a Muslim?* you might be thinking. Well, the answer is simple: you will need Muslims around you to help guide you as you learn your new faith. We can't do it all in one book, even though we want to. You will also need living, breathing people around you encouraging you. We wish we could be there with you every step of the way. But unfortunately, Allah has not made us omnipresent. We are barely present where we are actually present. Caffeine helps.

The Prophet (PBUH) said:

126

A good friend and a bad friend are like a perfume-seller and a blacksmith: the perfume-seller might give you some perfume as a gift, or you might buy some from him, or at least you might smell its fragrance. As for the blacksmith, he might singe your clothes, and at the very least you will breathe in the fumes of the furnace." (Narrated in *Bukhari* and *Muslim*)

His point was that friends rub off on each other. Having Muslim friends will help you become the best Muslim you can be. So, where do you get these new friends, you may wonder? You can pick your new Muslim friends up wherever Muslim friends are sold! Seriously, if you are trying to make new friends (and you should be trying to make new Muslim friends) just go where the Muslims are. And where is that? The falafel house of course! Oh yeah, and the *masjid*. Now that you are in the know about *masjid* etiquette, you can dust off your Friday best and head down to the *masjid* to pick up a few Muslim friends.

But, wait! Not all Muslim friends are created equal. Well, maybe they are *created* equal, but some are not going to be as good for you and your new faith as others. Some are too extreme, some are only Muslim in name, and some are just right. You might be tempted to hang with the "only Muslim in name"-type Muslims because things are new, and you want to take it slow–and you should–but this crowd will stunt your growth in faith. You will know the "only Muslim in name" crowd by their un-Islamic actions and even their comments about your conversion. The "only Muslim in name" Muslims will say something along the lines of "I should be taking lessons from you. You are more righteous than me since you are new, and all your sins are forgiven."

While this is true–you *are* new, and your sins *are* forgiven–you are not a role model ... yet.

You have a lot to learn and if a Muslim friend needs to learn Islam from you, they are probably not practicing their faith. And that is a problem. You don't want to hang with Muslims who don't take the *deen* seriously; they won't have much to offer. The "only Muslim in name"-type Muslims are also likely involved in *haram* activities. And likely, they will encourage you to continue your *haram* activities instead of encouraging you to give them up. They don't think pleasing or coming nearer to Allah (SWT) really matters and that is unfortunate for them, and a catastrophe for your new faith. This is bad company plain and simple.

Now you are probably thinking, "Gawd! You're not my dad! You can't tell me who I can and can't be friends with!" As true as that may be, you can think of us as your older sisters who have been down that road and been burnt and only want to see you succeed.

On the other end of the Muslim friend spectrum are the hard-line Muslims, who we will refer to heretofore as the "hard-liners" because it's fun and they would probably hate it. If you have a lot of zeal about Islam after you first convert, as many of us do, you might be tempted to hang with the hard-liners. They know the faith inside and out and you are gonna want to soak up as much info as you can. And you should! But this crowd will have you burnt-out before you can say, "*Asalamu Alaikum*". You will know the hard-liners by their willingness to judge everyone. And when they find anything (even things imagined or gossiped about) wanting in someone else's faith, they will deem those being judged (basically everyone except themselves) as "not

Muslim enough."

One of their favorite hobbies is to discredit Islamic scholars–people who have an entire lifetime of knowledge more than they do–just because they hold an opinion the hard-liners dislike. The hard-liners will expect you to be a perfect Muslim the day after you convert. This is not only an impossibility, it is also unfair and a standard to which no one can measure up to.

It is not that these people should be avoided like the plague and you cannot be friends with them, but we are saying you need to be aware that you shouldn't take your religion from the only-Muslim-in-name type of Muslims or the hard-liners. As a new Muslim, you may be looking to any Muslim as someone who knows more than you and to emulate even a little bit. These guys are not that.

A good rule of thumb: if you feel like your Muslim friends are pushing you too hard or, conversely, are pushing you to continue your old *haram* habits, they are not the examples to follow. The Muslim friends that you want are those who give you a little bit of info at a time, and who encourage you as you improve yourself and try to learn and implement Islam in your life. The "just-right" Muslim friends are there to answer questions about Islam. They never judge you when you are not quite ready for something, and celebrate your growth as a Muslim.

But wait a minute, not everyone lives near a big Muslim community and can be picky about their Muslim friends. So true. So wise. However, there is a new-fangled contraption called "the internet" where converts can often find Muslim friends in chat rooms, Facebook groups, etc. If this is your avenue to Muslim friends, know that the same rules above apply.

And before you go out into the brave, new world of Muslim friend-making, know that making close friends with people of the opposite sex is a recipe for heartbreak and it's inappropriate. Seriously, no Muslim man cozying up to a new female convert has ever had honorable intentions. They just don't. Period. Ever. Never ever. And convert brothers, sorry to say: you aren't going to be able to find a Muslim sister who wants to be your super close bestie friend. They have lives.

This is not to say that you can't get advice or ask someone of the opposite sex stuff or even say "*Salam*" or "hi" to them. It's just that attraction and feelings get in the way of friendship with a person of the opposite sex. You're not looking for a marriage partner; you are looking for a friend.

## TALES FROM THERESA TOWN

It is a hard story for me to talk about for many reasons. It brings back bad memories and puts me and my family in a suspect light. But I know that people can benefit from the lesson of Omar Hammami's journey and death. It is a cautionary tale. Many people try to paint him with broad strokes. The FBI called him one of their most-wanted. CNN called him a Jihadist rapper. Fellow *jihadis* call him a hero; those were the same people who murdered him. He called himself *Abu Mansoor al-Amriki.*

To me, Omar Hammami was a kid. I met him when I was first introduced to my husband-to-be. In those days, Yusuf (said husband), Omar, and a few other young brothers travelled together in a pack. Omar, while one of the youngest pack members, was often the loudest, and most energetic. A scraggly-bearded teenager in *thobes,* Omar was a frequent guest in my home where he would chat for countless hours with my husband, share meals with us, and on occasion eagerly offer his help when we were in a bind. He was a good friend to my husband and me.

Many say he became radicalized after 9/11, but the process was much slower and began far before that infamous date. Omar was not a man who snapped; he was not a sociopath. Omar was bright, magnetic, and passionate about Islam and wanted to help the Muslims in any way he could. But Omar was also extremely frustrated. After converting to Islam in high school, Omar felt increasingly isolated and lonely in his small town in Alabama where Islam was something most people had never heard of. Omar became increasingly angry: he was angry about what he saw as the lack of morals in American society and a lack of enthusiasm in his fellow Muslims.

His frustration and anger only grew when he faced bigotry and stereotyping after 9/11. The Iraq war and hearing his uncle's tales of being tortured in a Syrian prison also had a profound and detrimental effect on Omar. All of this led Omar to take a path of harshness. He became increasingly anti-American and forgot about the gentleness of Prophet Muhammad (PBUH) with people who were ignorant of Islam. He missed out on the wisdom behind the verse: "To you your religion and to me mine." (Quran 109:6) He failed to remember the patience that all Prophets had when faced with the same feelings of isolation and frustration.

After high school and having entered college, Omar decided he needed to get married. Having no success in the small Islamic community in Mobile, Alabama, he moved to Canada where he had a marriage prospect. My husband and I lost touch with Omar when he moved to Canada. We only heard through his family that he married and moved to Egypt, and from there to Somalia. In reading his autobiography, I found that Omar's feelings of isolation and frustration never subsided. Instead, Omar became increasingly blinded by these feelings and his own zeal. To him, there were no shades of grey. Things were either Islamic and good or un-Islamic and evil. He forgot that he once didn't have Islam and he himself needed patience and guidance from others. Omar never learned to see people as inherently flawed and complex. He saw them as either ultra-religious Muslims or disbelievers. He lost sight of the mercy and kindness of Islam and replaced it with force and fervor. He lost sight of the balance Islam demands.

Omar became the perfect mix of an impassioned, angry, and frustrated young man. This is a mixture that many extremists seek out and use to manipulate young, eager Muslims. Omar became the perfect prey. His migration to Somalia surprised many people. But what he did next was even more of a shock. Once in Somalia, he joined a terrorist organization called *Shabaab*. Omar became indoctrinated in their cause and was made to believe that by joining *Shabaab* he was helping to defend innocent Muslims. But, *Shabaab* had other aims in mind.

Ultimately, Omar woke up to *Shabaab*'s lack of adherence to Islam and questioned their legitimacy. Seeing that *Shabaab* instated heavy taxes on the already impoverished people in Somalia–and used these taxes to live lavishly–Omar spoke up. Hearing *Shabaab* teach their combatants that killing innocent civilians was allowed, Omar had enough. This was the end of Omar's affiliation with *Shabaab*. He learned that *Shabaab* was not interested in setting up an equitable Islamic government where its citizens could be safe and live in peace. He learned that they were a group that wished to establish more tribalism and inequality. But it was a lesson learned too late for Omar.

Reports of Omar Hammami's death cropped up every few months in Somalia, only for him to resurface a short while later. But a US terrorism expert who closely follows the inner workings of *Shabaab* said he thought the reports of his death in 2013 were accurate. It was true. We had mourned his death many times over. Each time a report of his death would hit the news, Omar would pop up again on YouTube or Twitter to say the claims of his death were false. After September of 2013, no one heard from him. Omar had been murdered by *Shabaab* for speaking out against them.

In exposing *Shabaab*'s un-Islamic practices, Omar also exposed groups like them who claim Islam while tossing its teachings out the window. He showed the world that these groups use Islam as a tool to manipulate people and then twist Islam to serve their own agenda. Omar had a good heart and a sincere desire to help Muslims. He wanted to be a man of action, but he forgot patience is a noble action. He wanted to follow Islam strictly, but forgot to be compassionate to others. He lost the balance of Islam and fell prey to extremism because of the "friends" he made, who used him and his good intentions. Our friends can have a huge impact on our lives. Choose them well.

# 13- Sex, Marriage, & Love

You might be shocked to find that we are broaching a topic like sex. Sex, as it is framed in some other faiths and cultural mindsets, is something that is to be done only begrudgingly and only with the sole purpose of having children. And because of our inheritance of this Puritanical attitude in some Western cultures, many of us who identify as religious have been raised with an unhealthy dose of mixed emotions when it comes to sex: shame, intense desire, more shame, and buried emotions.

Islam is different. Sex is recognized as a biological need, even beyond the need to procreate. Sure, having children is one of the functions of sex, but sex in Islam is also recognized as a means to attain pleasure and connection with one's spouse. And that is a very good thing, a necessary thing. Islam affirms that we all have sexual needs that are natural and healthy, and those needs shouldn't be buried under a mountain of shame. We shouldn't be embarrassed to talk about sex. Even though many Muslims have adopted this shame-based attitude, the Prophet (PBUH) was never one to shy away from talking about sex-education or sex within the framework of mutual pleasure in marriage.[13]

---

[13] There are numerous *hadith* to support this claim. One example: A female companion covered her face and asked the Prophet

However, like everything else in Islam, sex needs to be approached with wisdom and balance. Islam teaches us that we should not approach the fulfillment of any need outside of the limits set by Allah (SWT). To borrow and amend a phrase from *Spiderman*: with great pleasure comes great responsibility. Sex provides us great pleasure, but it also has the very real potential to harm us, and therefore, we must be responsible about it.

You are probably aware by now of how sex affects lives. Even if you haven't participated, you can look at those around you. Sex, and the lack of it, affects us emotionally, physically, and financially. We have to be real about what goes on in a sexual relationship. There are strong, deeply-rooted emotions attached to this act and consequences that are potentially life-altering.

Allah (SWT) says in the Quran, "And do not approach unlawful sexual intercourse. Indeed, it is ever an immorality and is evil as a way." (Quran 17:32) The emotional, physical, and financial pitfalls attached to unlawful sexual intercourse (sex outside of marriage) are the stuff that makes something a sin—doing something that harms oneself. Allah (SWT) doesn't just tell us something is a sin for the fun of it. He doesn't declare things sinful because it hurts Him in some way either. We cannot affect Allah like that, even if we wanted to. We don't have that kind of power. Sins are just the things God is telling us to stay away from because they harm us and are the pitfalls in life. It's easy to remember when you

---

(PBUH), "[...] Does a woman have a discharge [during sex]?" He replied: "Yes, let your right hand be in dust [may you prosper], how does the son resemble his mother?" (Narrated in *Bukhari*) Even though the woman asking the question was embarrassed, the Prophet was not embarrassed to answer.

consider that harm is a part of the word "*haram*."

The Prophet (PBUH), said, "Whoever among you is troubled by his sexual urge, let him marry - for marriage causes the eyes to be lowered and safeguards the private parts." (Narrated in *Bukhari*)

Islam, as a path to living life with the least amount of heartache, guides us to put sex in a healthy and safe context, wherein each party has rights and a backup plan. Like eating, praying, or any other act, sex has its time, place, and etiquette within the Islamic framework—namely, marriage.

Within a marriage, Islamically speaking, sex can be whatever pleases you and your partner, with the exception of anal sex[14] or sex during menstruation and postpartum bleeding.[15] Other than that, do whatever you like and feels good to you both. And, yes, whatever kink you prefer is fine as long as your spouse likes it too and you are not doing anything explicitly *haram*. Allah says in the Quran, "Your wives are a place of sowing of seed for you, so come to your place of cultivation however you wish and put forth [righteousness] for yourselves. [...]" (Quran 2:223)

We wanted to talk about sex here in this book because we want to give you some serious advice about marriage. For many of you, needing to have sex and wanting to do it in a *halal* context will be a driving factor for you to seek out marriage. And there is no shame in that. Men and women are made in this way, to feel a need for one another for this very reason: to become partners in life and love. But marriage in Islam is not like marriage in other faiths or cultural contexts.

---

[14] "The Messenger of Allah said: 'Allah is not too shy to tell the truth' three times. 'Do not have intercourse with women in their back passages.'" (Narrated in *Ibn Majah*)
[15] Quran 2:222

The Islamic marriage contract acts as a protection for individuals in a relationship. The marriage contract creates an environment within the marriage relationship where each party is protected from egregious harm that can come out of love, sex, and procreation. You sign the marriage contract to make sure you both agree to give one another your rights. And if those rights are not fulfilled, you will be held responsible by God. If you get a legally binding marriage contract (which we *highly* recommend), you will be held responsible under penalty of the law in your country.

The marriage contract protects you from a lot of drama. We have contracts drawn up when we buy a car or enter a business relationship in order to protect both parties' interests, but those contracts are only protecting our money and assets. Yet, somehow many think that a contract when it comes to sex–and more importantly, marriage and love–is callous. The romantic notion that "love will see us through" is a nice thought (which reality largely disproves). But emotions fade, while contracts are smart and lasting.

The Islamic marriage contract is kind of like a prenuptial agreement that is mandatory because we can lose sight of our needs, giving up too much of ourselves and our rights in the name of "love" and keeping the family together." But signing a contract does not mean that a marriage is only a contractual obligation and robotic in nature. Once that contract is signed, then you can allow yourself the natural emotions that come from intimacy and sex, knowing you are protected. You can then focus on building trust and a stronger emotional bond that goes beyond

137

sex, nurturing feelings of love and commitment to one another's well-being.

Allah (SWT) tells us that our spouses are like garments for us (Quran 2:187). This verse is alluding to sex, but it is also alluding to so much more. Like any good garment, marriage should shield you, support you, and make life more comfortable and even bearable when conditions are extreme.

## WHAT IS LOVE?

The emotional bond of marriage that we must nurture is a sign from God:

> And one of His signs is that He has created for you spouses from amongst yourselves so that you might take comfort in them, and He has placed between you love and mercy. In this there is surely evidence (of the truth) for the people who carefully think. (Quran 30:21)

However, sometimes this emotional love can go out of the bounds set by Allah (SWT), just like sex sometimes happens outside of these same bounds. Allah guides us to do everything with wisdom and balance. So, as a way to protect ourselves from the dangers of a love that goes too far, we must also learn how to love while seeking nearness to Allah. The Prophet (PBUH) said: "Allah will ask on the Day of Judgment: 'Where are those who loved each other for the sake of My glory? Today, - on a day when there is no shade but mine - I shall shade them with My shade.'" (Narrated in *Muslim*)

For some of us, this is a tough concept to understand. We come from cultures that teach us that, while sex is a game, love is the ultimate thing to worship. You know the sayings and songs: She/he "did it all for love." Romantic comedies, replete with their emotional porn, have us thinking that putting anything before love seems crazy, but this is just not reality (also actual porn has us thinking that our partners should look and act a certain way, which is also not reality).

But when you understand what it means to love someone while seeking nearness to the Owner and Creator of love, it makes loving for the sake of love sound insane (because it is). If you love your spouse for her/his own sake, you will start to see her/his flaws and ultimately be disappointed by her/his fallibility. Instead, understand Allah (SWT) is the only perfect Being and that He created your spouse exactly as he or she is, flaws and strengths, for exactly what he or she is meant to be and do, perfectly flawed. And so, everything you love about your spouse should make you love Allah more for creating him of her this way, or creating the circumstances that made him or her who she or he is.

Loving a person for their sake alone is like loving a painting and not crediting the painter. It was Allah who made all our lovable aspects. Shouldn't we love Allah for that? Shouldn't we love Allah for making our spouse smart, or funny, or sexy, or kind, or all of the above? This doesn't mean we can't love the painting. It just means we need to give credit where credit is due and love the painter for the painting, not vice versa. It means we put our love for God before our love for others.

It is also important to understand that we do not create love, nor do we put love in each other's hearts. You will probably be familiar with this concept if you have ever loved someone who didn't love you back, and did everything you could do to attain that love, but never could. We don't make love happen. We can't put love in our hearts or anyone else's. The

139

Prophet Muhammad (PBUH) taught us that not only is Allah (SWT) The Owner and Creator of us, our hearts, and love itself; He is also the One who controls our hearts. The Prophet often supplicated (made *dua*) calling Allah "The Turner of the Hearts."

If you have ever woken up one morning feeling no love for someone you had previously loved the day before, for no reason, you might get the concept. You are not in control of how you feel. This can help you understand where love comes from and who is responsible for it. If you were to believe that your spouse was the one responsible for your love, you might be utterly destroyed if his or her feelings for you waned or changed, as is only a natural occurrence and fluctuation in the course of a relationship. And you would do anything to make him or her happy and feel love for you (this is worshipful love—or putting your spouse before Allah (SWT)).

Understanding that Allah (SWT) is the owner of love and is in control of all our hearts will create a stable foundation, some perspective, and wisdom when it comes to love. So, instead of riding the feverish rollercoaster of love–becoming besotted or devastated with every smile or every fight–we can draw nearer to Allah. We can supplicate to The Turner of the Hearts to make our love for each other and Allah firm in our hearts.

Beware of love for the sake of love. It is indeed a kind of insanity that has the potential to destroy you. You need to know what healthy love looks like. You have to know that healthy love can be a means to achieving Allah's (SWT) pleasure, coming nearer to Him, and bringing peace and contentment into your life. While unhealthy, obsessive, worshipful love of your spouse (or anyone or anything), will be your

140

destruction, and the destruction of your heart.

## SOULMATES

Another Western construct that many of us converts have picked up is that of "soulmates." Some of us are under the impression that there is someone out there that will make everything OK, someone that will complete us (insert *Jerry Maguire* reference here, then begin eye roll sequence) and bring us happiness for the rest of our days. Where do we even get this from? It's completely made up. And it is also a form of worship.

Only Allah (SWT) is perfect. Only our nearness to Allah can make us feel complete, happy, and at peace: "For without doubt in the remembrance of Allah do hearts find satisfaction." (Quran 13:28) No one in this world will be the perfect puzzle piece to fit into your life and make you whole. A belief in this will only make you bitter from disappointment.

There will, *inshaAllah*, be someone that Allah (SWT) has willed to be your mate in this life that has so much in common with you and *does* bring you joy, and fills some of the blank parts of your life. But not in the ultimate perfect and fictional sense as with the concept of soulmates. Even the person Allah has willed for you to be with will cause you pain at times, and will need some refinement to fit into your life— just as you will cause them pain and will need refinement to fit into theirs. Relationships are built and maintained on a solid foundation of a common goal(s) (perhaps making it to *Jennah*?), compromise, and understanding. When we approach a relationship thinking that someone will be perfect, we will NEVER find that perfection.

However, Islamically speaking, there is such a

141

thing as soulmates, but it's not what pop-culture teaches us. It is not that we meet someone and realize we are perfect for one another and live with each other in a paradise here on earth. Our soulmate is the one with whom we work together to be as perfect as is humanly possible here: fulfilling each other's rights, having a satisfying sexual relationship, taking care of each other's emotional needs, seeking nearness to Allah (SWT), and advising each other.

And if you do all this, you will be with your spouse again in actual paradise—*Jennah*. Your literal souls will meet again in a perfect home with your Creator. True romance is wading through the imperfect life of this world together, fighting off all the traps of this world, having each other's back, being a comfort and companion to one another, and fulfilling each other's sexual desires—all so you can find each other again in the perfect world of *Jennah*.

Soulmates are earned. Romance is earned. Good and safe sex is earned. A happy marriage is earned. We have to work to make it what we want and be OK with the imperfect parts. This world is not paradise. But Allah (SWT) does give us all the tools we need to make life awesome here and then to reach perfection in the Hereafter. We just have to use those tools.

YOUR MARRIAGE RIGHTS

We have included, for your reading pleasure, a simple list of the rights you have as a husband or a wife. You can also add anything you want (that is not *haram*) to your marriage contract if it is something you would expect and need from your marriage and do not find it in the list of basic rights. This is your right as someone entering into a legal contract as a spouse: to add things to the marriage contract.

142

For example, if you know that you will need to have exactly three cats, a trip to Spain every five years, and have your spouse answer the phone for you when you don't want to, tell your intended spouse, and if he or she agrees, throw that in the contract so that it's legally binding. These are silly examples, but you need to seriously think about what you want in your contract.

Sister, do you want it written that you will not be prevented from furthering your education or having a career? Brothers, do you want to never have to live in a certain country or city? Ask your intended spouse if they are cool with it. If so, put it in the contract. Sign on the dotted line. Consummate your commitment. And start working toward happily ever after. If they are not cool with it and it is a deal-breaker, move on to the next candidate, no drama, no baby momma/daddy nonsense, no fighting over who gets the plasma TV and the fish tank. That's the great thing about not getting emotions and finances and sex involved before a marriage contract is written and signed. If one potential mate cannot give you what you know you cannot do without, it's easier to pass and find someone more suited to you. And *then* get started on sharing, loving, and building a life.

MEN'S BASIC RIGHTS IN MARRIAGE:

1.  The right to sexual fulfillment, assuming his wife is not ill, menstruating, having postpartum bleeding.[16] And no, you cannot force your wife to have sex with you.[17]

---

[16] Quran 2:222

[17] The Quran states that the marital relationship is to be based on love and affection (2:187, 30:21, etc.). Rape is incompatible with this. And scholars throughout Islamic history have classified rape as a

143

2. If a couple is blessed with children, the man has the right to have those children nursed[18] and raised well, if not by the mother, then by someone of the mother's choosing whom he pays[19] and she manages.
3. The right to be treated with respect, kindness, mercy, and compassion.[20]
4. The right to be respected in regard to whom is allowed into the home when he is not there.[21]
5. The right that his wife be fully and completely faithful to him alone, barring all other men.
6. The right to divorce, called *talaq*.[22]

It is important to note that despite what some cultures may dictate, there is no *ayah* (verse) of the Quran, or an authentic *hadith*, that states a man has a right to a wife who is also his full-time maid and cook. Couples need to work out between themselves who will be responsible for maintaining the home. Division of labor in a family is important and when left unaddressed it can put too much burden on one spouse or another, leading to resentment. You are in a partnership. You are adults. No one is obligated to feed you and pick up after you. And if someone does do these things for you, it is completely out of love and you need to respect and appreciate that whether

---

form of terrorism/violent crime/societal harm (*hiraba*).
[18] Quran 2:233
[19] Quran 65:6
[20] Quran 2:187, 30:21, and more
[21] "Their (husbands') rights over you (wives) is that you do not allow anyone whom they dislike onto your bedding and you do not allow anyone whom they dislike into your house." (Narrated in *Tirmidhi*)
[22] Quran 2:226-227

it is a wife or a husband doing it.

WOMEN'S BASIC RIGHTS IN MARRIAGE:

1.  The right to full and complete financial maintenance for herself and any children the couple produces in the marriage. All of their food, shelter, health care, and clothing needs must be provided for. Notice we said *needs*, not wants.[23] Though, gifts between spouses are highly recommended.
2.  The right to be maintained in a similar way to which she is accustomed. A man cannot take a woman who grew up in a very posh lifestyle and put her in his ancestral village with no running water and expect this means her rights are fulfilled, unless she willingly accepts this arrangement.[24]
3.  The right to sexual fulfillment with her husband, assuming her husband is not ill and is consenting.[25]
4.  The right to keep all her own money, both earned and inherited/given, without as much as an implication she should "help" her husband pay the bills, unless she herself willingly chooses this high form of charity. She doesn't need his permission or even his acknowledgment of how she spends her own money; though, mutual

---

[23] Quran 2:233 and 65:7
[24] "[...] Their rights upon you are that you should provide them with food and clothing in a fitting manner" (Narrated in *Muslim*)
[25] The Quran states that the marital relationship is to be based on love and affection (2:187, 30:21, etc.). Rape is incompatible with this. And scholars throughout Islamic history have classified rape as a form of terrorism/violent crime/societal harm (*hiraba*).

communication is always a good thing.[26]

5. The right to be given her *mahr* (wedding gift) in full before the death of her husband or the dissolution of the marriage bond.[27]
6. The right to be treated with respect, kindness, mercy, and compassion.[28]
7. The right to justice and equality in polygyny should she choose to be in a polygamous relationship, and it is legal in the country in which they reside.[29]
8. The right to divorce, called *khul*.[30]
9. The right to full maintenance of her physical needs for shelter, food, and clothing during her *iddah* (waiting) period, or the time between when they divorce and when she is permitted to seek out another spouse.[31]

This is by no means an exhaustive list of the rights of spouses. As always, we encourage you to do more research and know thy sources, context, and proper translation.

---

[26] Scholars agree that Quran 4:4 applies to all matters of women's financial independence.
[27] Quran 4:4
[28] Quran 2:187, 30:21, 4:19,
[29] Quran 4:129
[30] Quran 2:229
[31] Quran 2:241

# 14- The Marriage Question for Sisters

Many people believe that those of the same faith have to have the same opinion on everything, always. This nonsensical way of thinking is especially applied to Muslims by non-Muslims in the West. But we are members of a religion made up of billions of people, and we all have different perspectives.

Rather than feed into this nonsense—as united as we are on everything else we have presented in this book—we decided to be honest about our different perspectives in this chapter. We disagree about what you should do about the common pressure to get married right after saying *shahada*.

Kaighla says, "Absolutely not! Don't do it. Back away slowly—or, better yet, run from any proposals coming your way, sister. You do not have enough information about Islam to know how to protect your rights, and it's probably not going to go well for you."

Theresa says she feels uncomfortable telling sisters what to do, even though she knows getting married soon after *shahada* is super hard, and for some, it might not work. But for Theresa and several of the convert sisters she knows, it did work.

So, in our disagreement, we decided to just yell at each other, snatch out each other's weaves, and stop talking for months on end. Just joking. We for real didn't do any of that because we don't wear weaves, we aren't clichés, we like to practice good Islamic manners, we like each other, and we know our way around communication in a relationship.

We still love and respect each other even though we differ in our opinions, like bosses. So, we settled our difference of opinion on marriage for new sisters by deciding to tell you our stories and give you all the advice our experiences have afforded us.

## CANDID KAIGHLA

When I came to Islam, I had a one-year-old son. I was living in a Muslim boarding school with him, teaching English. Things were not exactly picture-perfect is what I'm saying.

So, about 5 minutes after I said the *shahada*, the people I worked with began pouring down advice and friendly reminders on me about how this and that was *haram* and how important it was that my baby grow up in a family unit. So, the marriage proposals started. Men who had never met me or seen my face began asking my boss about marriage to me. They knew exactly two things about me: I was a white American, and I was a new convert to Islam. Thank God someone stepped in and offered to be my *wali* (or "guardian," an older, wiser man who can help you discern the true character of a man and help you decide who is best for you, as well as stand by your side after the marriage in case things go sour), and I wish I would have listened to that kind man.

I met the "Milksheikh" on a marriage website for Muslims, because I wanted to be the one in control of choosing a spouse and my options were pretty limited in that community to very, very cultural

148

brothers with no grasp of what Islam looks like in America. The "Milksheikh" said he was a.) divorced. b.) had five kids in Egypt and c.) was a professor at a college in NYC.

As it turned out, none of those things were true. Without dragging you through all the gory details, I married that man, against the advice and concerns of my *wali* and his family. This man was actually not a professor at all, but a *sheikh/imam*, or something like a preacher in Islam. He was responsible for leading the Muslims in his care, and he was supposed to be a role model. In the most serious way I can tell you: he failed. But I didn't know that then, and I assumed that if he was a *sheikh*, surely, he must be a good role model to follow. So, I listened to everything he taught me, without much questioning. He must know better, right?

It didn't take long for him to begin emotionally and spiritually abusing me. Suddenly, my name was bad, my son's heritage was bad, my ways and mannerisms were bad. Everything about me "needed" to change so that I could be the "perfect" *Sheikh*'s wife. Then, by the time I learned about his wife in Egypt (whom he had never actually divorced), I had already quit my job in Chicago and moved to NYC to be with him. My son and I had nowhere to go.

Two years later, after my first child with him was born, we moved to Egypt so that he could be fair to his other wife and children (something which was my idea in the first place) and things became unbearable, quickly. But I held on for four years of hellish abuse, neglect, and hurt in that strange country with no family support.

Seven years and three children after I met him, I finally walked away from that man—but not without

149

a fight. He tried to deny my right to *khul* (or wife-initiated divorce) and even attacked the character of my friends who tried to stand up for me. Less than two weeks after our divorce, he was on a plane to Canada, leaving me and our children alone in Egypt with only my former in-laws to look out for us. Behind all our backs, he had married yet another woman, and continues his trend of abuse and neglect of new Muslims to this day.

Had I taken 2.5 seconds to learn anything about Islam and how I didn't have to be the quintessential Arab wife to be a good Muslim wife, I would have seen his tactic long before we married and avoided all that pain. Had I known my rights as a second wife–or even that I was a second wife–I'd not have given him a moment's consideration, something he knew and admitted was the driving reason behind his epic lie.

THIS IS MY ADVICE:

Spend as much time as you possibly can building your understanding of the religion before you even consider the possibility of marriage to someone, especially someone from another culture, like most Muslims in America are. You cannot imagine the struggles that intercultural marriages come with, and when you throw in the dynamics of a new religion for one person and an old for the other, things can get crazy.

Now, I am the last person alive to tell you not to marry at all, or not to marry a good man who has been cleared by your *wali*. I am a happily remarried mother of four, after all, and I waited the minimum three months after my divorce (the *iddah* time, or waiting time prescribed for a divorcee) to get remarried—no more, no less.

But before you even consider a man, don't get ahead of yourself. Were you totally game with marrying a man you had only met a handful of times before you were Muslim? No! So, don't imagine that tactic will go off without a hitch now that you are. Being Muslim does not, in any way, protect you from life's hardships, and a marriage to a stranger is a hardship on steroids.

Before anything, make sure you have the basics of prayer and belief down-pat. Make sure you know how you feel about things and make sure you can stand on your own two feet when someone tries to tell you their way is the only right way.

And when you feel super-confident in those things, seek out a *wali*. Maybe, like me, you have a few Muslim friends and one of their fathers agrees to take on the job. If not, I encourage you to actively pray night and day for that man to come along, as he will be the wall protecting you from being wooed and tricked by countless men. I'm not saying that you aren't smart and savvy when it comes to picking a mate. It's just that you may not be used to the tricks many so-called Muslim men like to pull. And having someone watching your back, like a *wali* will, never hurts. The harsh reality is that too many Muslim men in the world are Muslim in name only, and it is often easier for your *wali* (usually an older man) to see through a potential mate's façade or detect anything that he might be hiding from you. Before begging God for a husband, beg God for a *wali* to help you choose a husband, and the offers will come rolling in. Make it known in the local Muslim community that you are looking for a *wali*, and see what Allah (SWT) will do.

**A word on Muslim Matrimonial Sites:** Don't do it.

There is a 98.99% chance that the type of person you could meet on such a site does not have pure intentions. I met several men on such sites, including the Milksheikh, and every single one of them turned out to be frauds. Likewise, many of my friends have had their lives ruined by people they met on these sites. The cold fact of it is that the anonymity of a screen enables people–typically men–to coerce women into relationships with the types of men they would well-avoid in a real-life situation.

## TALES FROM THERESA TOWN

Immediately after I converted, I was asked, and asked, and asked again if I wanted to get married. My answer was no, and no, and no, thank you! I was young, still in school, and fearful of commitment (not because I was a player, silly—I just found that the thought of commitment made me itchy). This lasted for about a month.

Ok, so let me tell you a little bit about myself so that you can understand the weight of my situation. I was raised with several siblings but spent most of that time napping or by myself in my room. As an adult, I once spent (ok, regularly spend) weeks alone in my apartment without speaking to anyone or leaving and it didn't (doesn't) faze me. I am a (lovable?) curmudgeon, a raging introvert, a hermit, all of the above; whatever you want to call it.

But after I converted to Islam, I started to feel deeply, painfully, and utterly alone. "Lonely" is a sad and weak word incapable of expressing the intense emotion I was experiencing. My father passed away on my first *Eid*. And my mother had passed away a few years before that. A close relative suddenly cut off ties with me. I started wearing *hijab* and felt like a duck out of water in all my old circles. My Muslim friends all had Muslim families to commiserate with and keep them busy. My one convert friend moved away.

For the first time in my life, I actually wanted to have someone around to confide in, someone who could understand my situation. So, I got a cat. Because people ... bleh. Am I right? But cats get it.

Unfortunately, my cat didn't solve my problem. It's like she didn't even want to listen to me or be my bestie. Loser! I think Allah (SWT) put this intense feeling of utter alone-ness in my heart that I have never before, nor since, felt, so that I would seek out my husband. And that was exactly what I did one month after I converted: I started to look for my companion. It wasn't easy. I went through suiter after ridiculous suiter. One was too cultural. One was too shady. One was too much into the patriarchy. One already had a wife. The process was horrible, eye-opening, even heart-wrenching. A few of these "brothers" tried to take advantage of my lack of knowledge of Islam. But, *alhamdulillah*, I had some awesome sisters looking out for me.

Then, what seemed like a million years but was only a few months later, I met and married my husband (also a convert to Islam). It was the April after my November *shahada*. I thought I could finally relax and just be happy, but like all false senses of security, that was exactly where the adventure really began.

### LIFE AFTER MARRIAGE

It has been hard work from day one. Any marriage that has a chance requires two people who are willing to get down to the emotional, physical, and spiritual work. I'm talking give-me-five-more-push-ups-before-you-vomit work. The bare minimum you must expect from a relationship is that both people are: doing their best to seek nearness to and love of Allah (SWT) and doing the work of the relationship, whatever that means at any given moment.

The basis of my marriage is, and has always been, Islam. Even though this doesn't automatically make a relationship happy or strong, Islam gives us the instructions and parameters in which to operate for optimal results. My husband and I look out for each other on every level—physically, emotionally, spiritually, etc. We share the burdens of life and the relationship. We want Allah (SWT) to be pleased with us, so we recommend each other to do our best. We want to be successful in this life and the next, so we follow the steps of the Prophet (PBUH). The most you can expect from a relationship is that the work you do brings you joy in this life and ultimate joy in the next.

THIS IS MY ADVICE:

If you get married soon after converting, make sure you do these six things:

1. You know your rights as a Muslim woman and a wife.
2. Base your relationship on Islam.
3. Be willing to be as patient as a flipping saint, as it were, while never allowing your spouse to oppress you in any way.
4. Know what loving someone for the pleasure of Allah (SWT) is and learn how to do it.
5. Don't diverge from the list of deal-breakers

154

below.

6.  Do your background check on him.

But I also recommend that you find someone who is a convert to Islam like yourself. Not everyone will be able to do this because there are a ton more female converts than male converts, but I have found that no one can relate to you like a fellow convert can. Being able to relate, knowing what each other is going through, having the same cultural understandings and references, being able to understand each other's family and be a fellow Western Muslim representative to them is such a great asset. I'm not saying that intercultural relationships are a no-go. But I am recognizing that they do bring extra challenges. However, even if you do decide to look for a fellow convert to Islam when you are ready to get married, all other advice still stands.

## MUSLIM WOMEN OF COLOR

We fully recognize that your experience may be very different from ours. We know that a lot of the experiences we've had hinged on our shared, generally Caucasian, racial heritage. And this experience might be vastly different for you if you are from a different racial heritage. Unfortunately, Muslims are people, and some heritage Muslims and even white converts have some seriously disgusting prejudices. We are all a sisterhood, a brotherhood based on faith. And there is zero tolerance for bigotry in Islam. Know that without a doubt. But, as you are aware, people have been known to suck. We sincerely hope that race is not an obstacle to anything, marriage or otherwise, for any of our sisters. But we know that the struggle is real. We would desperately love to give advice here for the sisters who might come across issues of this nature. We wish we could say that it is more like the advice we give to the brothers or like this or that. But we do not presume to know this experience, as we are not women of color and have not walked in their shoes. We would be absolutely gutted if we were to give some bad advice based on our lack of knowledge and cause any of our sisters harm.

If you are a woman of color who has come to Islam and you are currently struggling to find a husband, or even if you aren't, and have experienced some indignities from ignorant Muslims, please know that you have a right to call people out, to push for change, to complain to your Lord about your oppressors. Our Prophet (PBUH) told us to "Beware of the supplication of the oppressed for there is no barrier between it and Allah." (Narrated in *Bukhari*)

We have done our best to take as many different experiences and perspectives into account in this book as we have worked with a beautiful array of converts over the years, but we sincerely apologize for any places where we might have a blind spot. We are fallible. But we do feel fairly confident that the rest of the advice in this chapter is standard for all.

FINDING THE RIGHT SPOUSE

Even though we disagree on some things when it comes to the marriage question for sisters, and we have had very different experiences, we do agree on a lot of things. And we have some cohesive advice on what to look out for when you do begin looking for your spouse.

Some new Muslims have rose colored glasses on

right after they convert. They might even go as far as to think all Muslims are like the Prophet (PBUH) or his companions. This is not true today. Not all people who call themselves Muslims strive to be like the Prophet and his companions. Some don't know what being a good Muslim means, and some just don't care. Islam is perfect—Muslims are decidedly not.

Before you even consider getting married, read the *Seerah* (the life of the Prophet-PBUH) so that you know the basics about Islamic manners and how a Muslim man is expected to treat you and act in the world. And consider the following deal-breakers:

## DEAL-BREAKERS

**He already has a wife.** We don't care what anyone tells you: polygyny is no picnic. There are very, very few times polygyny has worked in a 21$^{st}$-century, Western context. And when it does, it's because the man was of extraordinary character and the women knew about one another and were also of extraordinary character. Whatever lines he feeds you about it "not being necessary" that she knows, whatever he says about her being "OK with it," don't believe a word unless and until you sit down with her personally–or on the phone–on multiple occasions and come to understand her true feelings on the matter. A woman whose husband has gone behind her back to take another wife is a woman scorned ... and that is a deal-breaker.

**He doesn't pray five times a day.** It does not matter if a man is from the direct line of Prophet Muhammad (PBUH): if he doesn't pray five times a day, he is not the man for you. A man who doesn't even do the bare minimum of worship will stunt your growth as a Muslim, like the Chinese footbinding of yore stunted the growth of countless women's feet. Don't imagine you will be able to make him religious, either. A Muslim woman is forbidden, for good reason, from marrying a non-Muslim.[32] If he doesn't give Allah His rights and due respect, he will not give you your rights or your due respect. Do not marry a man who is not at least practicing Islam at the bare minimum. He will use what he thinks are his rights over you to oppress you and then not give you any of your actual rights. That's a deal-breaker.

**He drinks alcohol and parties.** A Muslim man who has no shame in drinking alcohol is not a Muslim man you want in your life. Yes, he may be a practicing Muslim, but if he is drinking alcohol or doing other such drugs, he is not serious about coming closer to Allah (SWT). Marriage will not stop him doing the *haram*. And this type of *haram* always leads to other types of *haram* and drama. That's a deal-breaker.

**He was cool with dating you before you were Muslim.** We are absolutely overwhelmed with the number of women who have come to us seeking guidance on this issue. It always starts the same: "I love him. He's my *habibi*. He says he wants to marry me. He said he already told his family about me. We're serious. But ... he doesn't want me to be Muslim or wear *hijab*, and he refuses to tell me when we will marry." Frankly, that man is using you–for what, we don't know (ok, yes, we do)–but he does not actually care for you, and he is not being open with you about his true intentions. That's a deal-breaker.

**He is religiously harsh and demands you become perfect overnight.** If a man walks into your life and

---

[32] There is no guarantee that the Muslim wife of a non-Muslim man will receive her Islamic rights.

says that, if he were to marry you, he would decide how much you cover yourself, he is not the sort of man you want or need in your life. Muslim women observe modesty to please Allah (SWT), not their husbands or fathers. This sort of man will likely expect you to–and in some cases, force you to–be as superficially Muslim as he is without allowing you to grow spiritually. He will not allow you to learn, understand, and incorporate Islam at your own pace. You will have to have all that done tomorrow. And that is not Islam and that is not OK to expect from anyone. Do not marry a man who is callously religious. That's a deal-breaker.

**He demands that you change your name, take his last name, or generally become part of his culture.** Hear us clearly: there is nothing inherently contradictory between Western culture and Islam. You are a Western Muslim. Whatever your culture is, God put you in that culture for a reason, and he gave you the family you have for a reason. As we discussed in earlier chapters, God doesn't want you to give up your identity. He wants you to improve your character. If Allah (SWT) is not asking you to give up your identity, no one can. That is a deal-breaker.

**His family wants to control your life/make you their slave.** Speaking of the cultural Muslims, remember that if you marry a man from another culture, even if he is game with learning where cultural mores end and religious edicts begin, his family may not be. Your in-laws may have expectations of you that you are not OK with. In some cultures, the new daughter-in-law becomes a kind of servant to the family. This has nothing to do with Islam, and in many cases, is seriously oppressive.

But even if your in-laws don't expect servitude, they may expect you to act, walk, or talk a certain

159

way. While you owe your in-laws respect, you do not owe them obedience. Your husband will have to do what his parents say, within certain limits—just like you need to do what your parents say, within limits, even if they are not Muslim. But he cannot expect you to obey his parents, and vice versa. And if he is not going to shield you from his parent's abuse or cultural expectations, that's a deal-breaker.

If you are a new brother reading this, most of these deal-breakers apply to you as well ... except the whole worry about hidden polygamy.

IF HE MEETS THE PREREQS

If you find this gem of a human being, you should also know that you have to be attracted to him. If you don't like the look of him, you will have a hard time fulfilling his rights on you. Who wants to have sex with someone they are not attracted to?

Once all these requirements are met, talk to people in the community about his character, and not just his friends, but people who have worked with him and people who have seen him down and out. Find people who might not like him and ask them why.

Check out his online presence. See if he is up to perverted or shady stuff. Let him meet your family and ask what they think about him (taking any prejudice your family may have into account). Checking him out is not being unromantic or sneaky; this is how it is done in most cultures in various ways, and this is how it needs to be done to protect yourself from less-than-savory characters. This is your life, girl: be smart about it.

Once you have sniffed around to check out his character, then make sure he isn't going to make you move somewhere you are uncomfortable with going.

Make sure he will not make you quit your schooling or career. Make sure he will support your ambitions. Discuss with him what he expects from you as a wife. Tell him what you expect from him as a husband. Talk about children, division of labor in the house, the standard of living you both expect. Find out if he's interested in having more than just you for a wife, and how he would go about things if polygyny is his thing and you are cool with that. And get all of the stuff you agree upon in your marriage contract.

Whether you should get married right out the gate or not is up to you. But let us just say: if you do decide to get married soon after conversion, you better be big time aware of who you are marrying, what they expect, and what your rights are in Islam. And, sister, demand, we repeat, DEMAND your rights from Day One so these brothers know they aren't dealing with someone they can take advantage of.

Sister, you might think you can skip the next chapter: "The Marriage Question for Brothers." But don't be so hasty. Before you flip to the following chapter, take a moment to check out the sections entitled "Marry a Woman for Her *Deen*" and "New Muslim Brothers Making Marriage Difficult on Themselves." These bits of wisdom apply to you as well.

# 15- *The Marriage Question for Brothers*

To marry or not to marry? Let's face it: that is *not* the question for many of the new Muslim brothers. If you are not already married and of marriage age, the reality is that you need to find a wife and you need to start looking now. Unless you want to and absolutely know that you can be celibate.

If you have or will read the chapter entitled "The Marriage Question for Sisters," you might notice the stark contrast in the advice we are giving to brothers and sisters. There is a very good reason for this: new Muslim women often fall prey to the many, many unsavory Muslim men in the marriage market. So, it is best for the sisters to take their time, get to know their rights, and make a careful decision.

We recommend you do the same: take your time, get to know your religion, and make a careful decision. But unfortunately–or fortunately, however you look at it–you are not thought of as prey to unsavory Muslim women. In fact, you will most likely have a hard time finding a spouse in the Muslim community, hence the advice to begin your search soon (while you learn all you can about Islam and marriage within the Islamic framework).

The reason it is difficult for new brothers to find a suitable spouse in the Muslim community is because many Muslim families are suspicious that new Muslims are insincere or about to leave Islam. As a man, many Muslim families who come from patriarchal societies will think of you as a potential leader of the household. And if apostasy is a possibility, you are not going to be considered a viable option for their daughters. Even if you are not under suspicion of apostasy, Muslim families might steer clear of you because of the cultural influence they believe you will have on their daughters.

The only reason this doesn't apply to new sisters is because Muslim families think their sons will enforce their culture and Islamic standards within the marriage. And they are not wrong. Their sons have been sometimes known to enforce Islam right out of the new sisters' hearts and destroy their sense of self. And this is the same reason we caution sisters to beware.

You are not subjected to the same kind of oppression. You have a different kind of oppression to watch out for. Please note that not all Muslims or Muslim families think like this, but it is a serious issue, nonetheless.

You would be right to think this suspicion some fellow Muslims have of new brothers is unfair and closed-minded. We agree. It's pretty messed up, and it's even *haram*. Allah (SWT) tells us in the Quran, "O ye who believe! Avoid suspicion as much (as possible): for suspicion in some cases is a sin [...]." (Quran 49:12)

Muslims are supposed to be one community. We

163

all have cultural differences. And every single one of us runs the risk of apostasy, no matter what religion our families follow. But these are the cold, hard facts about the marriage market you are getting into. Muslims are people and have their faults and hang-ups. Muslims oppress each other, even though Islam dictates the opposite.

We want to prepare you. But don't let it impact your faith. If you face this kind of issue in your search for a spouse, don't give up. You don't want to be in a family with this kind of attitude anyway. And as long as you do your best to be conscious of Allah (SWT), you are a very viable option for marriage. You are not scraps, as some people may falsely assume.

And so, we recommend that you start the search for a Muslim spouse early. Put the word out in your new community that you are interested in marriage. Let people know what you are looking for in a spouse. Talk to the *imam* of your local *masjid* about marriage. Tell him you are in the market, and ask him if he can keep an ear out for you.

### New Muslim brothers making marriage difficult on themselves

On the other side of the coin, sometimes new brothers make finding a spouse hard on themselves. You might be one of such brothers and if you are, you will need to let go of your notions of what a perfect wife should look like, act like, think like, etc. There is no such thing as perfect. Women aren't one-dimensional creatures who are supposed to serve you, and look perfect for you, and only have sexual desire when you want them to.

No woman ever has left her life as a model/medical doctor/Islamic scholar and gladly

164

abandoned her ambitions, all to lie in bed waiting for your command and bearing your children (when she is not cooking gourmet meals and cleaning, of course), all while miraculously stopping the aging process.

We have seen brothers wait years and years for this fictitious creature to come along. Sorry to break the news if you weren't already aware, but women cannot, by the very nature of being human, be perfect. Even if you were to actually find a woman who came close to this perfection, would she want you? Are you also a model/medical doctor/Islamic scholar with no ambition other than pleasing her)? Unfortunately, some men have a sense of entitlement in this way. And it is in this way that they oppress themselves. We know you are not like that, but we just wanted to make sure we covered all our bases in advice-giving.

Keep in mind that the Prophet (PBUH) himself married women who were older than him, divorced, widowed, had children, etc. And, yes, this advice also applies to the sisters. We aren't just being hard on the dudes here. No one is allowed to expect perfection from others and not expect the same from themselves on our watch.

### MARRY A WOMAN FOR HER *DEEN*

The Prophet (PBUH) said:
> A woman may be married for four things: her wealth, her lineage, her beauty and her religious commitment. Seek the one who is religiously-committed, and may your hands be rubbed with dust [may you prosper]. (Narrated in *Bukhari* and *ibn Majah*)

The Prophet (PBUH) knew what men would be

165

looking for in a wife, but he also knew that none of those things really matter in the long run except a woman's *deen* (faith), because a woman committed to her faith will be the best partner in this life and the next.

Yes, you need to be attracted to a woman in order to marry her. Who wants to sleep with someone they are not attracted to? And, as a husband, you will be required to please your wife's sexual needs. But that does not mean she needs to be without physical flaws.

Yes, it would be nice to marry a wealthy woman and to have some financial stability. But it is still up to you to provide for her, no matter how much money she has. So, marrying a woman for her wealth makes no sense. And yeah, sure, it would be nice to marry a woman with a good family. Who doesn't want to be related by marriage to the Queen?

To be clear, the above reasons (wealth, good looks, influential family) are not deal-breakers. If a sister is super-hot, rich, well-connected and she follows the *deen* AND she wants to marry you, LOCK IT DOWN! Just don't make a woman's wealth, lineage, or beauty the only things you look for in a spouse.

When you make finding a religiously committed woman a priority–*the* deal maker or breaker–you are looking for someone who will have your back. You are looking for someone who will be patient with you. You are looking for a partner who has great character, someone who is ride-or-die. You are looking for someone who will concern herself with gaining religious knowledge instead of wealth and material things. You are looking to be partners with someone whose good habits will rub off on you.

If you narrow your search for a wife to a woman who is conscious of her Creator, you will be a co-parent, *inshaAllah*, with someone who will be a good

166

example to your children. If you look for this kind of person, you will have someone in your life who will do her best to fulfill your needs, take care of you, and (hopefully) gently remind you to do the same for her so that you can both grow nearer to each other by coming nearer to Allah (SWT). You will have someone you can work with to become soulmates. All this applies to you too, sisters! You aren't getting off that easily.

## *MAHR* MATTERS

Another important thing to think about when the question of marriage arises is your money situation. The first thing you need when you decide on a certain sister is the marriage gift, something a man must give to his wife upon signing the marriage contract. This is called the *mahr* and it is your obligation and your wife's right. Allah says, "And give the women [upon marriage] their [bridal] gifts graciously [...]." (Quran 4:4)

Your intended spouse has the right to ask for whatever she feels is appropriate for her marriage gift. The *mahr* is for her protection in case you are ever not in the picture any more, for one reason or another, and she is finding it difficult to provide for herself. Historically, women around the Prophet (PBUH) asked for anything from the groom accepting Islam or saying the *shahada,* to large amounts of gold. The *mahr* can be anything or any amount your future-wife asks for (but, there is a difference of opinion on this that we are not going to get into).

The Prophet (PBUH) advised his companions who were not wealthy to give the *mahr* to their new wives, even if it was small. He said, "Search for something, even if it is just a ring made from iron." (Narrated in

167

*Bukhari* and *Muslim*) There is a balance in the marriage gift, as with everything in Islam. While a woman has a right to ask for any amount or anything for her *mahr*, a man should not be expected to give something that is outside of his capability. You can also compromise with her and agree to give her part of the marriage gift at some point in the future. But please do not ever agree to pay a *mahr* that will make you go into debt. If a sister demands a higher *mahr* than you are capable of giving her, and she is inflexible in this, you have to think seriously if she is the right woman for you.

## BE PATIENT

Be patient with the search for a spouse. Remember that Allah (SWT) has planned someone to be your wife. If it isn't working with one sister, and the next sister's *wali* is giving you grief for cultural reasons, and yet another sister wasn't feeling it, remember that there is no reason to get down. Those sisters weren't meant to be your wife.

Allah (SWT) had a plan for you long before you were born. You might not get His plan when things seem difficult, but His plan is perfect and when you look back in the years to come, you will find the ultimate wisdom in it. So, don't sweat rejection. And don't approach the *haram*. You are a great guy and the right person will come along. Trust in Allah.

## TALES FROM THERESA'S HUSBAND'S TOWN

After converting to Islam at the age of 16, I (Yusuf–Theresa's husband) was warmly welcomed into my local Muslim community. Going through my teenage years as a member of the small but tight-knit Muslim community in the ('merican) South, I felt as if I belonged. I felt at home in the *masjid* among my brothers and sisters in faith. That was until I decided it was time to get married. The fathers I approached about marriage to their daughters literally laughed in my face at best or patronized me with a pitying look at worst.

Let me back-up a bit. I was determined to do everything to the letter of what I thought then was the law. So, that meant an arranged marriage, which meant the terrifying prospect of asking fathers about their daughters, whether they were interested in getting married, and what they might think about marrying me. And that is where the laughing in the proximity of my facial region happened.

It was the worst-case scenario, but I thought it was the only way. I still think this was the best and most respectful way to go about finding a spouse for me, but I also know now that there are other ways that work for other people that are equally appropriate, as long as the rules of Islam are followed.

And so, I was met with laughter. But I brushed it off. I told myself it was because I was a broke 22-year-old. I told myself it was a normal reaction, even a rite of passage, if you will. But I knew it was more than that. I knew it had a lot to do with what they "lovingly" called me, "redneck", something that was hurtful to me. I was not from what would be considered a "good" family. I was not from their culture. I had my ups and downs in faith since converting, especially during my impressionable teenage years when I was trying to balance being a Muslim living in a non-Muslim household. And no, I was not from a wealthy family, nor was I a professional with an advanced degree and a large paycheck at the time. So, I was deemed unsuitable.

169

But I had more to offer than being a part of a certain culture or family. I had more than money. I had a dedication to my faith and the sincere desire to be a good husband. Despite being turned down time and again, I knew I needed a partner. I needed to be married. I didn't want to commit *haram*. So, I broadened my search. I prayed and made *dua* incessantly for Allah (SWT) to provide me with a good Muslim wife. Little did I know my wife had not yet converted to Islam. It was going to take a little longer.

I approached fathers who were converts themselves, thinking they would have compassion for my situation. They did, but their daughters were not interested in marriage. I expanded my search to communities surrounding me, to women who were twice my age. I was not concerned with looks, or age, or even the chance to have children. I just wanted and needed companionship. I needed a partner. Little did I know, at this point, my future wife had just converted, and those same feelings were stirring in her heart.

I kept praying. I kept looking. I kept making *dua*. I kept talking to aunties, and uncles, and brothers, and cousins, and *imams* about prospects near and far. I even decided that, if I couldn't get married, I would adopt a cat to ease the loneliness.

Then, I started having dreams about a woman who would become my wife. In the first dream, I saw a woman standing before me with her hand on her hip giving me a playful smile. I will not describe her here out of respect for her modesty, but I will say that after marrying my wife I realized that the dream was true. In the next dream, I was in a tall building without exterior walls, overlooking a beautiful landscape of rivers and gardens. The same woman

170

from my first dream was bathing in a tub and asked me to join her. I refused and said that I was fasting. Immediately after saying this, the sun dropped out of the sky, she grabbed me, and I woke up. In the third dream, I saw the same woman again who along with a different woman were both attached, from the waist up, to the body of a cow. They told me that when one was skinny, the other was fat and they alternated before my eyes. Eventually, the woman that would not become my wife separated from the cow, grew legs of her own and walked away preoccupied with something interesting. Only my wife-to-be stayed behind. I still don't know what the last dream meant, but I included it anyway to be thorough and tell the complete story. In hindsight, maybe it represented the years of alternating hardship and ease that my wife and I would have together in the early years of our marriage. Allah (SWT) knows best. These dreams came to me before I had ever communicated with or even heard of Theresa. But these dreams gave me hope.

In my waking life, I faced one rejection after another and was getting desperate. I was begging Allah (SWT) almost hourly for a good wife. I had such a deep emotional and biological need to be married and I utterly refused to seek what I needed outside of marriage. I drew strength from the story of Prophet Yusuf (Joseph PBUH). When he was tempted by a beautiful, wealthy woman, he chose prison over committing *zina*. Since it is *halal*, I even started considering marrying a Christian woman.

I was losing patience in finding a Muslim wife. Little did I know, the literal woman of my dreams (who is right now rolling her eyes at the phrase "woman of my dreams") lived two hours' drive away from me, had just come to Islam, and was about to contact my best friend's mother about marriage prospects.

It was about five months into my search for a spouse that I met Theresa. It felt like years of torment getting to this point. But we met and hit it off, famously. We had so much in common. We are from the same part of the world and somehow both found Islam. We are the same age. We have the same sense of humor (even though she is much funnier than I am). We had/have the exact same goals. And we were both desperate to find each other.

We both prayed *istakhara* (the prayer to ask for direction in life), told our families, and married in April of 2002, one month after meeting. None of the rejection and desperation matter now because I know it was a humbling experience that I needed at the time. And I know that had I married any of those sisters who had rejected me or whose families had rejected me, I wouldn't have married, learned so much from, and had so many amazing adventures with my wife. It was Allah's (SWT) plan for me, for us, and I would go through all the pain of the search again just to come out with this same result. Allah really does have a plan for each of us. We just have to trust Him and be patient.

## DEAL-BREAKERS

If you skipped the previous chapter, "The Marriage Question for Sisters", don't be so hasty. Before you flip to the next chapter take a moment to turn back and check out the section entitled "Deal-Breakers". This is a bit of wisdom that can be useful to you as well. For you, though, you won't have to worry too much about marrying a woman who is already married, but you knew that.

172

# 16- Dealing with Islamophobia

We are not going to sugarcoat this for you because you will find out soon enough (or, most likely, you have already known) that Islamophobia is real, scary, and intensifying in the West. It sucks being the scapegoat *du jour*. But it's nothing new for Muslims and many other minority communities. Fear of "outsiders" is as old as community itself.

The bad news is that as long as some influential politicians and lobby groups continue to profit off of war and just plain ole injustice, there will be an Islamophobic agenda in some groups of government and media. As long as the average Westerner lacks exposure to the correct information about everyday Islam and the average Muslim, there will be Islamophobia. As long as people who call themselves "Muslims" act un-Islamically, there will be Islamophobia.

But the good news is that the global Muslim population is growing. Words like *halal* (thank you, Halal Guys) and *hijab* (thank you, Muslim fashion designers) are becoming more and more mainstream. And so, the more people know about and are exposed to Islam and practicing Muslims, the harder it will be to cling to fear and hatred. The more we refuse to return hate and fear with hate and fear, the sooner Islamophobia will become a bad memory. The more we take the legitimacy of Islam away from groups like ISIS, the quicker they can be defeated, *inshaAllah.*

The University of California, Berkeley, Center for Race and Gender defines Islamophobia as:

> A contrived fear or prejudice fomented by the existing Eurocentric and Orientalist global power structure. It is directed at a perceived or real Muslim threat through the maintenance and extension of existing disparities in economic, political, social and cultural relations, while rationalizing the necessity to deploy violence as a tool to achieve 'civilizational rehab' of the target communities (Muslim or otherwise). Islamophobia reintroduces and reaffirms a global racial structure through which resource distribution disparities are maintained and extended.

Pretty intense, right? Read it again. It's dense and deserves a few readings. It's important to understand what's happening when it comes to Islamophobia, and when it comes to the inner workings of fear-mongering; otherwise we just kinda get lost in the rhetoric. If you don't know the cause, you can't tackle the problem properly.

UC Berkeley nailed it. Islamophobia has been around for a long time and has very deep roots that span centuries. It is not a "natural phenomenon" that comes out of tragedies like 9/11 and the advent of ISIS (as the Islamophobia lobby wants us to think). It works in the reverse order. It's a fear and hatred of a victim who might lash out because of an intentional

174

imbalance of power and resources. At its core, it is a fear of a people who have been oppressed, so keeping them subjugated is rationalized.

And so, when atrocities like 9/11 occur, the groups of government and media that create mass Islamophobia shamelessly use these tragedies to package and sell their fear and hate to the masses. Johnny Q. Patriot–whom the Islamophobes prey on in order to sell their fear and hatred–does not understand the deep historical, political, socioeconomic, and racial roots or the injustice that creates Islamophobia. All Mr. Patriot knows is that what happened on 9/11 and what is happening with ISIS is terrifying, and he must protect his family.

As the saying goes: if you knew how the sausage is made, you would never eat sausage ... or something like that. This is true of both sausage and Islamophobia. The average person on the street that has been sold Islamophobia has no idea how Islamophobia is made, and that's no mistake. Mr. Patriot would never buy into Islamophobia if he knew how it is made, if he knew that the families of the people he is told to hate have been degraded, starved, and murdered—all so the Islamophobes could have more stuff (oil) and power.

## WHAT DO YOU DO ABOUT IT?

Just because you understand the power grab that creates Islamophobia and the global context of this specific kind of hatred doesn't mean you must return that hatred and fear. We know as a fact that hate begets hate. And we are held to a higher standard as Muslims.

Groups like ISIS and Al Qaeda have taken it upon themselves to return hate with hate and have created more hate as a consequence. They have played right into the hands of the Islamophobes. They have been everything and worse than the Islamophobes say Muslims are, all by acting un-Islamically. Allah tells us in the Quran: "And not equal are the good deed and the bad. Repel [evil] by that [deed] which is better; and thereupon the one whom between you and him is enmity [will become] as though he was a devoted friend." (Quran 41:34)

When we follow this command of Allah (SWT), when we do more than just turn the other cheek, when we bandage the hand that smacked us, we teach people about Islam. How many former Islamophobes have become Muslim (or advocates against Islamophobia) because a Muslim returned their evil with a good deed?

But when we lack sophistication and wisdom, Islamophobia grows. How many people who were neutral about Islam and Muslims were sold on Islamophobia because of an evil deed of Al Qaeda or ISIS or their ilk? How many less-educated Muslims have left Islam because of the un-Islamic actions of so-called "Muslim groups"?

It's a simple equation, and it is up to each one of us to decide to follow the teachings of the Prophet (PBUH) and the Quran and to do better and be better. Or we can choose to follow the teachings of those who consider themselves our enemies. And we can choose to bring ourselves down to–or lower than–the level of the fear- and hate-mongers. It is up to each of us to help an accurate understanding of Islam grow through good actions, or turn people away through our bad actions. And we are telling you right now: you do not want to be responsible on the Day of Judgment for turning people away from even understanding Islam. That is so much more serious than a hundred heart attacks, no exaggeration.

## HOW A MUSLIM SHOULD ACT
## IN THE FACE OF ISLAMOPHOBIA

The first line of defense against the dark arts of Islamophobia is smiling. Smiling makes people feel at ease. It's contagious. It's *Sunnah*. One of the companions of the Prophet (PBUH) said, "I have never seen someone more in the habit of smiling than Allah's Messenger." (Narrated in *Tirmidhi*) And, best of all, it's charity.[33] As little orphan Annie sang, *smile or you are naked*, or something like that.

The other side of the coin is that a negative attitude is passed around like a cold in kindergarten. Going around mean mugging people and expecting to be discriminated against because you are (identifiably?) Muslim is a self-fulfilling prophecy.

According to a 2010 poll conducted by TIME magazine, 62 percent of Americans claim to have never met a Muslim.[34] Consequently, Americans are formulating their opinions about who Muslims are and what Islam is from the media and outspoken Islamophobes.

The best way to tell people about Islam is to show them Islam. Wave and smile at neighbors when they pass by. Share food with them and make sure they never go hungry. Look out for your neighbor's property. Remove anything harmful from the street. Always show patience toward others and have a cheerful attitude. You know ... act like a Muslim. Show people how Islam informs your actions as a Muslim.

And if people happen to ask what your faith is, let

---

[33] Fiqh-us-Sunnah, Volume 3, Number 98
[34]Altman, Alex. "Time Poll: Majority Oppose Mosque, Many Distrust Muslims." *Time.* Online.

them know if you feel safe enough to do so. Being a visible, respectable representative of Islam in your community can go a long way. The Prophet (PBUH) said, "Make things simple and do not complicate them. Calm people and do not drive them away." (Narrated in *Bukhari*)

In some instances, you will have the opportunity to dispel myths and misconceptions about Islam. Now, some Muslims will tell you it doesn't matter what people say about Islam: we know the truth and Allah (SWT) will judge. Sounds right, but it's not. The Prophet (PBUH) was sent as a messenger so that humankind could understand Islam correctly. If people have misconceptions about Islam, it is the Muslims', as inheritors of the Prophet's mission, responsibility to clear up those erroneous perceptions of Islam. It's not our job to convert people, but it *is* our duty to dispel and clarify Islam's message- God is One and He sent all the true prophets with this message of His oneness. Do this with stellar manners.

However, if you feel as if you cannot control yourself and have good manners, or if you feel unsafe or too new to speak up, that is totally understandable. You can, instead, support those who do speak up in whatever way you feel comfortable with.

If you feel like things are getting too crazy–and this may be a very real possibility at some point in the future as you are reading this book–and you feel as if you are no longer able to practice your religion in the country in which you reside, then *hijrah* is a real option. *Hijrah* is the Arabic word for migration. We should all be making *hijrah* to Allah (SWT), or doing our best to draw nearer to Him by doing the actions that please Him and leaving the actions that displease Him. But, from time to time, migrating in physical time and space from a place where Islam is hard to practice to a place where you are free to practice your religion is wise or even necessary.

There is a very real Islamic precedence for the *hijrah*. The Prophet (PBUH) lived in Mecca, his home and the home of his family and tribe for generations, until the pagan Quraysh made it so unbearable for the Muslims to live and practice their religion there that they had to make *hijrah* to Madinah. In fact, our Islamic calendar began when the Prophet made *hijrah* from Mecca to Madinah. As of 2018, the Islamic year is 1439-1440. That means it has been 1,439-1,440 years since the migration of the Messenger.

However, (and this is a big however) this doesn't necessarily mean that one *must* move to a Muslim-majority country. In many Muslim-majority countries, true Islam is hard to find and even harder to practice. According to researchers at George Washington University, countries with significant Muslim populations have overtly failed in embracing the values of their own faith in politics, business, law, and human rights.[35] This is a sad reality of the world in which we live. But that doesn't mean that Islam cannot be practiced in other countries. The only reason we mention this is so that you, bright-eyed and bushy-tailed new Muslim, don't get the impression that making *hijrah* to, say, Egypt, will make practicing Islam and your life in general easier. It probably won't.[36]

We have seen many a naïve new Muslim be chewed up and spit out by the corruption and un-Islamic environment of so called Muslim countries. If you do find yourself in a situation where you want

---

[35] McElroy, Damien. "Ireland 'leads the world in Islamic values as Muslim states lag'." *The Telegraph.* Online.
[36] Ask Kaighla. She tried that. Twice. And it failed. Epically.

to–or even need to–make *hijrah*; do your research, prepare, and look before you leap. And may Allah (SWT) be with you as you find and settle in a new home for His sake.

Leaving is an extreme option. But an option nonetheless. No matter what action you take, you should do your best to forgive. When the Prophet returned to Mecca with 10,000 troops in victory over the Quraysh (the pagan enemies of Islam) after making *hijrah* to Madinah, it was expected that he would exact revenge for the many years of torture and war that the pagan Arabs had inflicted on him and his followers. But he didn't. In an event that had never before and has not since been witnessed, Prophet Muhammad (PBUH) said:

> 'O Quraysh, what do you think of the treatment that I should accord you? They said: 'Mercy, O Prophet of Allah. We expect nothing but good from you.' Thereupon Muhammad declared: 'I speak to you in the same words as Yusuf spoke to his brothers. This day there is no proof against you; Go your way, for you are free.' (Narrated in *Muslim*)

No matter what grievances we have, none can be greater than the grievances the Prophet (PBUH) had against the Qurayshi enemies of Islam. Most of the Prophet's time here on Earth as a messenger was spent facing one obstacle after another placed in his path by the original and most vicious Islamophobes. He suffered insults, attacks, torture, boycott, starvation, and war—all to bring us this message of Islam. And it is with this example of forgiveness that we need to move forward and face the world.

In 2003, I lived for a short time in Savannah, Georgia, a town filled with tension. Everywhere I went I was reminded that I was enemy number one. I was flipped off, cursed at, and threatened. It came to a head one Friday when I attended *Jumuah* in a tent outside the charred shell of the *masjid*. The *masjid* had been burned down five days earlier. I can tell you that it is easy to start to hate people you fear. I hated the unknown assailants for making me feel unwelcome in my own country, for being so ignorant of Islam, and for making me feel like I had no right to my beliefs.

But I can also tell you that this mutual hatred has never solved anything. The more they hate me, the more I hate them, and so on until every single person suffers. The only way to break this cycle of hatred is to start understanding each other. To understand where we are coming from, to understand each other's goals, hopes, dreams, and so on.

I completely understood the fear the assailants felt. I was a non-Muslim on 9/11 and felt terrified that a similar attack would take my life or the life of any one of my loved ones. As someone studying Islam at the time, I also understood this kind of evil had no place in the faith of Islam. It might be that you, reading this book, were once someone who hated Muslims, but through this hatred you started learning about actual Islam and became a Muslim. Allah has a plan for all things even if they seem bleak. Allah says, "And [remember, O Muhammad], when those who disbelieved plotted against you to restrain you or kill you or evict you [from Mecca]. But they plan, and Allah plans. And Allah is the best of planners." (Quran 8:30)

# 17- Islam Should Make Your Heart Soft

By now, you've learned a good bit about Islam. And we commend you! By now, you've done a lot of hard work in cleaning out your life and adding good into it, *inshaAllah*. Congrats! You are truly on your way, *mashaAllah*. You may even start to feel good about all the Islam that you are living, and you should. But sometimes when people feel like they have their situation situated, they need to look outwardly. And in some cases, all this work and knowledge you've been doing and attaining leads to an ego trip.

The unfortunate fact of the matter is that many new Muslims fall into the trap of judging others once they feel like they have a handle on their new faith, and we want to warn you against this deadly (*iman*-wise, not physically) trap. The signs and symptoms of an Islamic ego trip may include, but are not limited to: swelling of the head, RJF (resting judgey face), nose stuck in the air, excessive eye rolling, impossible standards for others often combined with a tingling sensation when you think about how great you are.

If one or more of these symptoms occur, consult your Quran, and read, read, read. The Prophet (PBUH) said, "No one who has an atom's-weight of pride in his heart will enter Paradise." Upon hearing the Prophet say this about pride, someone came to him concerned that loving to wear nice clothing and shoes was a sign of pride. The Prophet (PBUH) explained that, "Allah is beautiful and loves beauty," meaning to love beautiful things and to look nice is not prideful. But, he continued, pride is "to reject the truth and to look down upon the people." (Narrated in *Muslim*)

If you truly have a handle on your Islam, it will make you humble. It will open wide your view of things and people. Islam will flood your heart and life with light and peace. Islam breaks down the barriers of race and worldview. It should make you give a Care Bear stare to the bad guys (even if they are also Muslim) and work for the best for every human being. It should not be inflating your ego.

## JUDGING OTHER MUSLIMS

So, for example, if you find yourself judging women who don't wear *hijab*–or don't wear it like you think they should–as being "less Muslim," you need to check yourself. The same goes for judging brothers without a beard. If you find yourself sure that anyone who listens to music (the *haram*-ness of music is debatable) must inherently not love the Quran, you need to take a step back.

At the very, very worst, these people you are judging need more faith and more kindness needs to be shown to them, including keeping them in your *duas*. What your fellow Muslims *don't* need is someone standing around pointing out how they are "headed to hellfire". That is not for you to say. It's not for any of us to say.

All that we can see of others is on the surface. We have no way of knowing what is in other people's

183

hearts. We have no idea what battles they are waging against their own desires. We have little information about the trials they are suffering. We have zero clue what amazing good they do behind closed doors. It is not up to us to judge others. It is our job to continuously work on ourselves and to offer kindness to others. And if we are successful in that, a side effect may be that we are a good example.

COVERING SINS & COMMANDING GOOD /
FORBIDDING EVIL

Pride is a kind of disease of the heart that convinces us that we don't need to do anything else to be better (something that is never true for anyone), that we are for sure deserving of paradise, and that other people need our criticism in order to improve. It is a delusion that cuts off introspection and self-awareness, and puts the focus on others. But here's the thing: we will always need to be working on ourselves. We will never reach perfection, what with being human and all. And none of us knows how Allah (SWT) views us.

We must remain between hope in Allah's (SWT) mercy and fear of His anger. None of us is safe from Hell and none of us is guaranteed Paradise. All we are guaranteed is an opportunity to do our best and ask for Allah's mercy when we fail. The best of the best people to have walked this Earth–after the Prophets, of course–were the companions of the Prophet Muhammad (PBUH), the men and women who followed and lived with Prophet Muhammad.[37] And there are many *ahadith* about them being downright

---

[37] "You are the best nation produced [as an example] for mankind. You enjoin what is right and forbid what is wrong and believe in Allah [...]." (Quran 3:110)

terrified they would enter Hell. Who are we to think we are on point?

When we start to think about judging others and harming their reputation, we need to know that the only reason *we* have a good reputation is because Allah (SWT) has covered our sins and has only shown people the good sides of us. And Allah requires us to hide the sins of one another, not to discuss them openly with other people and tear apart people's dignity. The Prophet (PBUH) said, "Whoever covers [the sins of] a Muslim, Allah covers [his sins] on the Day of Judgment." (Narrated in *Bukhari*) Sign us up for that! This is so important because so much of what facilitates our livelihood depends on our dignity and reputation. We must protect and shield each other in this way.

However, by now we are sure you have seen a pattern in all things Islamic. There is always balance. To be sure, we cannot go around judging people, treating others harshly, and exposing them because of some failing we perceive, because this is a sign of pride in us and it is damaging to others. But we also are expected to help our brothers and sisters by recommending them to do what is good and forbidding what is evil.

Allah (SWT) tells us that:

> The believers, men and women, are *awliya* [helpers, supporters, friends, protectors] of one another; they enjoin *al-Ma`ruf* [i.e., Islamic Monotheism and all that Islam orders one to do], and forbid [people] from *al-Munkar* [i.e., polytheism and disbelief of all kinds, and all that Islam has forbidden]." (Quran 9:71)

From this and the many verses and *hadith* like it, we know it is our duty to help a brother (and sister) out. But there is a difference between judging, exposing people's sins, and treating them harshly for the evil we think they do, and commanding good and forbidding evil.

And the difference is notable. Judging and treating people harshly is like demanding that someone allows you to watch how they brush and floss their teeth so that you can know if their oral hygiene is up to your standards, and, therefore, if you will permit them to talk to you. But commanding the good and forbidding the evil is like pulling your brother or sister in Islam aside and whispering to them that they have some food stuck in their teeth, and then offering them a toothpick so they can get it out if they so choose.

The judgey-harshness thing comes from a place of wanting to feel superior and is never deployed with manners or kindness unless it is to feel superior. While commanding the good/forbidding evil comes from a sincere place to help facilitate *Jennah* for your brethren and is always done in the best and kindest way possible. So, if you see that a brother is doing something grievously wrong, like praying to a statue (*shirk*) or something, it would be a great opportunity for you to:

1. Determine if a.) this bothers you because you know this is a grave sin and want to see this person in *Jennah* or b.) if you feel like this is a good opportunity to show off your knowledge.
2. If option a is your intention, then think of a kind and private way to explain the brother's error to him. If option b is your intention find a way to shut your ego down because you are just worshipping a different idol than that brother. Change your intention and think of a kind and private way to explain the brother's error to him.

3. Wish them well and don't judge them if they don't take your advice. Then make *dua* for them.

## *DAWAH* AND JUDGING NON-MUSLIMS

You've found and embraced the truth you've been searching for. Maybe you feel like everyone must know and share in this glorious knowledge! You must make *dawah*!

Whoa! Hold your horses, mate. Not only is it bad *dawah* to start "preaching" to everyone you know about Islam being the truth and that they have all been wrong, wrong, wrong—it's also really rude and unkind. Prophet Muhammad (PBUH) taught us that the true believer can be identified by the fact that his neighbors are safe from him. Of course, we can assume that the *sahabah* were not all rampaging murderers who terrified their neighbors, so what could he have meant?

The scholars say that this implies not only, yes, they should be safe from us hurting them physically or stealing from them, but also from our inconsiderate attitude, lack of respect for boundaries–of every type–and most of all, our tongue. Being a Muslim requires, without a shadow of a doubt, good manners. If you are approaching those you love about Islam because you truly care about them and their well-being in this life and the next, and not just because you want others to convert in order to validate your choice, know that telling people they are wrong and headed for destruction is not the way to get through to them. Did that approach work on you? Most likely not.

Allah (SWT) also tells us that that approach would not have worked on even the companions of the

Prophet (PBUH):

> So, by mercy from Allah, [O Muhammad], you were lenient with them. And if you had been rude [in speech] and harsh in heart, they would have disbanded from about you. So, pardon them and ask forgiveness for them and consult them in the matter. And when you have decided, then rely upon Allah. Indeed, Allah loves those who rely [upon Him]. (Quran 3:159)

If you do choose to tell people about Islam, or make *dawah*, because you love Islam and want everyone to have this amazingness in their lives, start by telling them about how and why Islam has changed your life for the better. Tell them about God's Oneness and that all the messengers from Ibrahim to Isa to Muhammad (PBUT) were brothers and brought one message from one God. Tell them about Allah's mercy and love for His creation. It is love for God that opens hearts, not threats of Hell.

After you give them the message of Islam, then leave them alone about it. Don't pester people about matters of faith. If you live Islam by example and have delivered the message, those who are interested in knowing more will ask. Also, know that it is up to Allah (SWT) to guide whomever He wills. It is not up to us to guide people. All we can do is deliver the message in word and action. The Prophet (PBUH) could not even guide whom he wanted. He made *dawah* for ages with one of his uncles and he never accepted Islam. Even though the Prophet's uncle knew Islam was the truth, he let his pride get in the way, and Prophet Muhammad could not force the pride out of his heart and replace it with Islam.

But the Prophet also didn't judge his uncle by Islamic standards. That is going to be key for you as well. Just like you shouldn't be judging other Muslims, you definitely can't judge non-Muslims by Islamic standards. It's unfair and unkind. They don't even know what the standards are, and they certainly don't know the wisdom behind them, and neither did you at one point. Islamically speaking, ignorance is an excuse for not obeying a law. If you don't know, you can't be held accountable. And beyond ignorance, all Islamic laws apply only to those who accept the message of Islam.

Be kind, be patient, and make *dua* for the guidance of the non-Muslims in your life. But don't judge. After all, Islam came as a mercy to humankind and it is on the shoulders of the Muslims, both raised and converted, to extend that mercy to all. Prophet Muhammad (PBUH) said that God does not show mercy to those who do not show mercy to others. (Narrated in *Bukhari* and *Muslim*)

If your Islam is making you harsh, unyielding, judgmental, rude, or downright mean, check again if it is God you're worshipping or if it might just be your ego. Islam makes people peaceful, humble, and gives them joy. Pride makes people cranky, judgey, and harsh. If you are showing signs of worshipping your ego, all you have to do is:

1. Stop.
2. Repent to God.
3. Ask Him to protect you and guide you.
4. Thank Him for hiding your flaws.
5. Extend that same mercy you hope for from God to everyone around you.

TALES FROM THERESA TOWN

Get your favorite monster-repelling blankey and pop some corn 'cause I am about to tell you a terrifying tale about the monster I used to be. *distant, eerie scream*

After converting, I found myself in the midst of a very friendly and accepting South-East Asian community. And because of my surroundings, I unwittingly fell into an Indo-Paki, *Hanifi* phase. Don't worry if you don't know what this means. I didn't either. And I do not regret it. The people who welcomed me into Islam were so great and I am forever grateful to them for teaching me so much and being patient with me.

But then one dark and stormy night (not really, it was actually a sunny day, but I gotta sell the horror story theme here) I up and moved to a different city with a very different Muslim community. I had no clue that the community I was about to enter was so different from the one I had just left. I didn't know Muslims could be so different.

I had stumbled into an overly strict interpretation of Islam. But, because of that, I learned so much about differences of opinions, innovation in religion, verifying sources, different sects and schools of thought from the contrast in the community and the wealth of knowledge that my new community had. I felt like I had gone from being Muslim-light to being thrown into the deep end of the pool of Islamic knowledge. It was intense, but I was game. And then *I* became intense.

As I learned seriously technical knowledge within the first year of my conversion, I also noticed that the members of my new community were using their knowledge as a weapon. It was almost as if they retreated during the day to dig into *hadith* and Quran just to bring their knowledge with them to beat someone over the head.

I witnessed sisters have a bitter and prolonged

190

fight over interpretation of minute details of the *Sunnah* and everyone ended up losing. It was insanity! I watched people come to Islam, get involved in this kind of battle of opinions, and leave Islam entirely. Their faith had turned into a kind of armor that was rigid and suffocating but necessary to defend themselves from the Muslims they kept company with. Their faith also became sharp and brutal but necessary in order to strike, offend, and make themselves feel superior.

I witnessed a child being treated with contempt because his recently converted mother was listening to music! This is oppressive! There was little compassion, no brotherhood, and little love for Islam and Allah (SWT). There were only rules as offense and defense. This is what happens when people harden their hearts. It's bleak but it is also contagious. I put myself in the middle of this sandstorm, and my heart became harder and I became harsher.

I was front-row witnessing brothers backbite each other because one's beard was not what they considered the "proper length". These standards are impossible! And I ended up holding harsh opinions of people who actually had good hearts, unlike me. I found any woman who didn't wear a Saudi style *abaya* to be immodest and not worthy of my time. I was insane! I thought less of people who had any different opinion than me. I was oppressive! I once saw a sister not sit down while she drank some water (it's a *Sunnah* to sit while you drink[38] or eat[39]) and I was as shocked as if I were watching her commit murder. I had impossible standards!

To be sure, there were people in this community

---

[38] *Tirmidhi.* Vol. 3, Book 24, Hadith 1879
[39] *Tirmidhi.* Vol. 3, Book 24, Hadith 1857

who had soft hearts and substantial knowledge. There were kind souls who only wanted to practice Islam, love Allah (SWT) and their brothers and sisters. I could have learned from these good and kind Muslim examples. But I chose severity, and the battle of the egos instead. And I became a monster.

I learned a lot, but I also un-learned the really important things, the things that Islam was revealed to give us: solace, fraternity, equality, joy, and ease. It was all lost. My heart nearly broke from the inflexibility and it took me a long time to heal from this experience. Being too strict is as bad as being too easy-breezy about your faith. Things that are too hard will break from brittleness, and things that are too soft will drift away from want of structure. Islam is the middle path.

# 18- *When in the Field*

A few weeks after taking *shahada*, new Muslims can start to feel overwhelmed and worried. There is so much information, so much to consider, and so many things to learn and do. Many new Muslims may wonder, "Did I make the right decision?" The answer is a resounding yes!

Nothing worth having comes easy. And Islam is the absolute best thing to have in this world. Period. As a new Muslim, all you need to do is what you can, one day at a time.

What you need to know when implementing Islam into your life is that the first revelations to Prophet Muhammad (PBUH) and his followers were not rules and regs. The first 10 years of revelations were about faith, the oneness of Allah and His majesty, love, and mercy. And then slowly, when this part of the message was firm in the believers' hearts, Allah (SWT) revealed to the Prophet (PBUH) what rules we should follow so that we will not harm our own souls. Islam was not a book plopped down on the believers; it was a process of revelation that lasted for 23 years.

And as a new convert, you should focus on learning the message of Islam, learning about Allah's (SWT) love and mercy, learning how to pray, and what the prayer means. In other words, you should implement Islam in the same way Allah revealed it to

His messenger (PBUH).

Allah (SWT) knows your situation. He knows your capability. And Allah knows that too much, too fast can lead to overload and burnout. That is why the message of Islam was not revealed in a day. And this is why you should only do what you can and learn little by little. Islam is not a sprint. It is a marathon.

Converting to Islam may mean that family members disown you, friends leave you, and challenges arise in your life. This is not unusual. All people who do great things have to go through trials. But the peace you obtain when you have Islam in your life is far greater than any fake friend or any test you face. When the trials of life get to you, remember the Prophets' challenges. Ibrahim (PBUH) was thrown into a fire by his own father. He was utterly alone, but in the best company with Allah (SWT) and the Angel Jibril.

Prophet Muhammad (PBUH) and his companions were considered outcasts in their clans. They were rejected by their society to the extent that their own families proclaimed themselves their enemies and boycotted them, insulted them, and tortured them. They had no friends but each other and Allah. Prophet Yusuf was imprisoned. Prophet Nuh (Noah) preached Allah's message to his people for 950 years, but only a very few followed him. Prophet Ayyub suffered almost every trial imaginable, but was still pleased with his Lord and his religion.

Looking to people who have suffered a great deal more than we could ever imagine puts things in perspective. Understand that hard times are a source of reward. Know that we are not the first to walk this

194

path, and that as long as we stay on this path, Allah (SWT) will not leave us.

## NEVER LOSE HOPE: ALLAH'S (SWT) DOORS ARE OPEN

Feeling overwhelmed, feeling alone, facing trials? Remember that you are on a spectacular path that not many people travel, not even many heritage Muslims. And for your struggle to become closer to Allah (SWT), Allah will come closer to you.

The Prophet (PBUH) said:

> Allah the Almighty said, 'I am as My servant thinks I am. I am with him when he makes mention of Me. If he makes mention of Me to himself, I make mention of him to Myself; and if he makes mention of Me in an assembly, I make mention of him in an assembly better than it. And if he draws near to Me an arm's length, I draw near to him a fathom's length. And if he comes to Me walking, I go to him at speed.' (Narrated in *Bukhari, Muslim, Tirmidhi, and Ibn Majah*)

If He has created you, and all that exists, and He certainly has, Allah (SWT) can surely get you through the times when you cannot see hope for the future. "[...] Be not sad, surely Allah is with us. [...]" (Quran 9:40)

## ALLAH'S (SWT) FORGIVENESS HAS NO LIMITS

When you first come to Islam, Allah (SWT) does not expect you to be perfect nor are you expected to know everything. Even the most devout and learned of people are still not perfect. But when you do slip up and commit a sin you know is a sin, you must also know Allah is the Most Merciful.

Prophet Muhammad (PBUH) said, "I swear by Him in whose hand is my soul, if you were a people who did not commit sin, Allah would take you away and replace you with a people who would sin and then seek Allah's forgiveness, so He could forgive them." (Narrated in *Muslim*)

Allah (SWT) knows we are weak. He created us this way so that we would return to Him and ask forgiveness. Thinking our sins are too great for forgiveness is limiting Allah's capability. And we know Allah is All Capable, the owner of mercy. Allah (SWT) tells us in a *hadith qudsi*:

> O son of Adam, so long as you call upon Me and ask of Me, I shall forgive you for what you have done, and I shall not mind. O son of Adam, were your sins to reach the clouds of the sky and were you then to ask forgiveness of Me, I would forgive you. O son of Adam, were you to come to Me with sins nearly as great as the earth and were you then to face Me, ascribing no partner to Me, I would bring you forgiveness nearly as great as it. (Narrated in 40 *Hadith Qudsi* and *Tirmidhi*)

### STAY POSITIVE AND NEVER GIVE UP

Being positive doesn't mean pretending that times aren't tough, or being in denial about your own suffering. Being positive means knowing that Allah (SWT) has the absolute power to change your situation. Being positive means knowing that living Islam can and will change your life in miraculous ways if you just keep going. You never know when ease is just around the corner.

Remind yourself often of what touched your heart about Islam and led you to bear witness that Allah

196

(SWT) is One and Muhammad (PBUH) is His messenger. Remember that any difficulty you may suffer, even if you stub your toe, Allah will reward you if you are just patient. Never lose hope in Allah.

Know that this life is just a small test with such an amazing and eternal reward if we just do our best to surrender and come closer to our Creator. Know that the good in life and the ease we experience totally outnumbers and outweighs the tough stuff. Don't forget that. We have so many blessings, but too often focus on the bad. Be specifically grateful for what you have. And know that while tests don't stop when one converts, peace will continue to grow in your heart as long as you seek your Lord. This is an amazing gift.

## CONTINUE SEEKING GUIDANCE

Muslims come in a wide variety. We are all different shapes, sizes, and sects. Many, many sects. It can be intimidating to know which way to follow when you are new ... even when you're not so new. There are probably many people telling you to watch out for these or those kinds of people. The Prophet warned us about this, saying, "whoever among you lives after I am gone will see a great deal of dissent." (Narrated in *Abu Dawud*)

You should for sure watch out for extremists. And we mean both extremes. Islam is the middle path. It's a balancing act of moderation. But, how in the actual world do you know you are on the right track when there are so many different opinions? Should you just throw your hands up in the air and give up on trying to find the true path Allah (SWT) sent to us? No, because that is weak and a total cop-out. Sorry to be so harsh, fam, but the truth is that letting yourself off the hook doesn't mean you are actually let off the

197

hook. We still have to answer to Allah (SWT).

So, what do you do? Be sincere and try. That's all. We ask Allah (SWT) for guidance and to keep our hearts open to it. Trust that God is the Most Merciful. Trust that He is the Utterly Just. Trust that He sent a message of egalitarianism and hope. Trust God. If anyone tries to tell you something about Islam that does to fit into this spirit, then know that is not Islam. Also know that beyond this, we don't get to say what truth and guidance are. We accept Allah's guidance even if it is not what we *think* we want. We for sure know you can do that because we are pretty sure that you didn't ever imagine that you would become Muslim. But when you saw the truth in it, you accepted it. Either you kept your heart and mind open, or Allah opened them.

Your journey isn't over. It is just beginning. Allah tells us if we are truly sincere in our journey to Him, He will certainly guide us, "[...] And whoever believes in Allah - He will guide his heart. [...]" (Quran 64:11) As Muslims, we make seeking guidance a priority in our lives. We do it at least five times a day. When we say *al-Fatiha* during prayer:

> You alone do we worship, and You alone do we ask for help. Guide us on the straight path, the path of those who have received your grace; not the path of those who have brought down wrath, nor of those who wander astray. (Quran 1:5-7)

Ask Allah (SWT), keep your heart open, and trust in Him. Who you gonna trust that is more trustworthy than Allah?

CONGRATULATIONS ON YOUR CONVERSION!

*MashaAllah*, Allah (SWT) guides whom He loves!

"Indeed, those who believe and do good deeds, the Beneficent will bestow love upon them." (Quran 19: 96)

If we have said anything good, true, and beneficial in this book; it is truly from Allah (SWT) alone. If we have erred in any way and said something incorrect, it is from our own selves. Please excuse us and ask Allah to forgive and guide us.

# Suggested Further Reading

*Being Muslim: A Practical Guide* by Asad Tarsin

*The Complete Idiot's Guide to Understanding Islam* by Yahiya Emerick

*Essentials of Islamic Faith: For Parents and Teens* by Suhaib Webb

*Halal Comfort Food: The New Muslim's Guide to Going Halal* by M. K. Johnston

*Hisnul Muslim: Fortress of the Muslim* A collection of supplications (*duas*) available for free online and as an app for iPhones and Androids

*The Islamic, Adult Coloring Book* by Theresa Corbin

*Reclaim Your Heart* by Yasmin Mogahed

*The Sealed Nectar: Biography of Prophet Muhammad* by Safiur Rahman Al Mubarakpuri, published by Darussalam Publishers

Sahih International English interpretation of the Quran available online at quran.com

*A Temporary Gift: Reflections on Love, Loss, and Healing* by Asmaa Hussein

# Glossary

## A

*Abaya-* A long, loose, robe-like dress, like a jilbab or a thobe.

*Abu-* A title meaning "father of." It is usually referring to someone's first born child. Abu Muhammad would be Muhammad's father. It can also be used as someone's nickname or kunya. Someone might be called Abu café as a kunya if he is someone who drinks a lot of coffee.

*Al-Fatiha-* The first chapter, or surah, of the Quran. It is composed of seven verses, or ayat. It is the chapter recited during the prayer or salah, asking for guidance and mercy from Allah (SWT). The literal translation is "The Opening," since it is the first chapter of the Quran.

*Alhamdulillah-* All thanks and praises are due to God.

*Al-Injeel-* The Gospel. The revelation Isa (PBUH) received from God.

*Allah-* God, the Creator. The only One worthy of worship.

*Allahu Akbar-* God is the Greatest.

*Amriki-* American

*Aqueeda*- Creed or belief. Correct belief is essential to the Muslim and it is outlined in the six pillars of iman. Believing in the six pillars of iman is having the correct aqueeda or belief in Islam.

*Asalamu Alaikum*- A greeting that means "peace be with you." The proper response is "Walaikum Asalam," meaning "and peace be with you."

*As-Suhuf*- The Scrolls. The revelations Ibrahim and Musa (PBUT) received from God and recorded in writing. They have since been corrupted and lost.

*Asr*- The afternoon prayer. It is the third of the five daily prayers.

*At-Taurat*- The Torah. The revelation Musa (PBUH) received from God in addition to As-Suhuf (The Scrolls).

*Ayah* (Plural: *Ayat*)- A sign from God. A verse of the Quran.

*Ayyub*- Prophet Job (PBUH)

*Az-Zaboor*- The Psalms. The revelation Dawud (PBUH) received from God.

# B

*Biddah*- Innovation in religion. Something added to the religion, by man, without divine decree.

*Bint*- A title meaning "daughter of." It refers to

someone's parent. Bint Muhammad would be daughter of Muhammad.

*Bismillah*- In the name of God.

*Bukhari*- A hadith collection collected by Imam Muhammad al-Bukhari.

# C

*Caliphate*- An Islamic state led by a Khalifa, who is a political and religious leader and a successor (khalif) to Prophet Muhammad (PBUH).

# D

*Daleel*- Evidence from the Sunnah, or an individual hadith. In the Islamic context, evidence can either be Maudu (fabricated), Daif (weak), Hasan (good), or Sahih (authentic).

*Dawah*- Explaining and inviting to Islam.

*Dawud*– The Prophet David (PBUH). Also, a collection of hadith collected by Imam Abu Dawud.

*Deen*- A way of life, religion.

*Dhuhr*- The noon prayer. It is the second of the five daily prayers.

*Dhu'l-Hijjah*- The twelfth and final month in the Islamic calendar. A sacred month in which the Hajj takes place.

*Dua-* Supplication or prayer asking God for something.

# E

*Eid-* Celebration. There are two Islamic celebrations: Eid al-Fitr, celebrated after Ramadan; and Eid al-Adha, celebrated after the Pilgrimage or Hajj.

# F

*Fajr-* The dawn prayer. It is the first of the five daily prayers.

*Fatwa* (Plural: *Fatawa*)- A legal opinion based on religious texts.

*Fiqh-* Literally means "deep understanding," refers to understanding the Islamic laws. Islamic jurisprudence based directly on the Quran and Sunnah that complements Shariah with evolving rulings and interpretations of Islamic Jurists.

*Fitnah-* Trial or test.

*Fitra-* The human being's natural disposition. In the Islamic context, it is the human instinct to worship Allah alone and know what is basically good and bad.

# G

*Ghusl-* The full body washing ablution/ritual cleansing required for rituals and prayers after menstruation or postpartum bleeding is finished, after one has had sexual contact with his or her spouse, or after one has experienced orgasm.

# H

*Habibi* (male)/*Habibti* (female)- Beloved. A term of endearment.

*Hadith*- A saying or tradition of the Prophet Muhammad (PBUH).

*Hajar*- Ibrahim's (PBUH) second wife. Ismael's mother. And the founder of Mecca. Many of the rights of *Hajj* and *Umrah* follow her footsteps as she became the founder of Mecca.

*Hajj*- The Pilgrimage to Mecca. The fifth pillar of Islam.

*Halal*- Permissible.

*Halaqa*- A religious gathering or meeting for Islamic studies.

*Hanafi*- One of the four schools of thought (madhabs) of religious jurisprudence (fiqh) within Sunni Islam. Named for its founder, Imam Abu Hanifa.

*Hanbali*-One of the four schools of (madhabs) of religious jurisprudence (fiqh) within Sunni Islam. Named after the scholar Imam Ahmad ibn Hanbal. The Hanbali madhhab is the smallest of four major Sunni schools.

*Haram*- Forbidden.

*Hijab-* The covering of one's body in loose, opaque clothing. For women, this includes everything but the face, feet, and hands. For men, this includes everything from the bellybutton to the knees.

*Hijrah-* Migration. The migration or journey of Prophet Muhammad (PBUH) and his followers from Mecca to Medina, or any migration of a Muslim from a place that is hostile to Muslims to a safer environment. It can also be a spiritual journey of coming closer to Allah (SWT).

*Hiraba-* Waging war against society or terrorism.

# I

*Ibn-* A title meaning "son of." It refers to someone's parent. Ibn Muhammad would be son of Muhammad.

*Ibn Majah-* A hadith collection collected by Ibn Majah.

*Ibrahim-* Prophet Abraham (PBUH).

*Iddah-* A woman's waiting period of three months after a divorce or death of her husband before she can be remarried.

*Iftar-* The evening meal that is eaten at the end of fasting. Iftar is eaten at sunset/Maghrib.

*Ihram-* The sacred state which a Muslim must enter in order to perform the major Pilgrimage (Hajj) or the minor Pilgrimage (Umrah). Also, the clothing men must wear during Hajj which consists of two, white, un-hemmed sheets.

*Imam-* A religious leader, not necessarily a scholar but one who is learned, leads the prayer, and gives Islamic advice.

*Iman-* Faith.

*InshaAllah-* God willing.

*Isa-* Prophet Jesus (PBUH).

*Isha-* The night prayer. It is the fifth of the five daily prayers.

*Ishaq-* Isaac. Ibrahim's (PBUH) second son.

*Ismael-* Ishmael. Ibrahim's (PBUH) first son.

*Isnad-* a chain of authorities who have transmitted a report (hadith) of a statement, action, or approval of the Prophet (PBUH).

*Isra and Miraj-* Two parts of the Night Journey that the Prophet Muhammad (PBUH) took during a single night around the year 621. The story is in surah al-Isra of the Quran and in the Sunnah. In the Isra part of the journey, Prophet Muhammad traveled to Masjid Al-Aqsa in Jerusalem. In the Miraj journey, he then ascended to heaven where he spoke to God, who gave him instructions to take back the details of prayer to the people.

*Istakhara-* A prayer said in order to ask Allah (SWT) for guidance to the correct action or path in life. It is two raka (units of prayer) and then a specific dua, called istakhara, that can be found in *Hisnul Muslim* (a book of dua).

# J

*Janaza*- Islamic funeral prayer.

*Jazak Allah Khairan*- May God reward you with good. Used to express gratitude. "Wai-yaki" is the correct response, meaning, "and to you."

*Jennah*- Paradise. Heaven. A place of utter perfection that the human mind cannot grasp.

*Jibril*- Angel Gabriel. This is the angel charged by Allah (SWT) with delivering Allah's guidance and message to all the prophets.

*Jilbab*- A long and loose-fitting coat, similar to the abaya or a thobe.

*Jihad*- A struggle in the way of God. The primary jihad one must perform is to fight against base urges that leads one to sin. The secondary jihad is to defend oneself or a Muslim country when it is being attacked for no other reason than the individual or the inhabitants of a country worship Allah (SWT) alone. It is often mistranslated as holy war.

*Jumuah*- Friday. It refers to both the day of the week and the congregational prayer at the masjid that happens on the day of Jumuah (Friday).

# K

*Kaba-* The cube shaped building in Mecca towards which Muslims pray. It has been said it was built by Adam (PBUH), and then rebuilt by Ibrahim (PBUH), and was the first building dedicated in the worship of God on earth.

*Kafir-* Disbeliever.

*Khalifa-* A title which means "successor" or "steward." It most commonly refers to the leader of a Caliphate- rulers of the Islamic empire after the death of the Prophet (PBUH). The last Caliphate ended in 1924.

*Khul-* A divorce initiated by the wife.

*Khushu`-* Focus, specifically when praying.

*Kufr-* Disbelief.

*Kufi-* A brimless, short, and rounded cap sometimes worn by Muslim men.

# L

*La illaha ila Allah-* There is no deity or god but the one true God- Allah.

# M

*Madinah-* A city in western Saudi Arabia. In the center of the city is the Al-Masjid an-Nabawi (Prophet's Masjid). It is the city to which the Prophet and his companions migrated after suffering torture and murder at the hands of the pagan Quraysh.

*Maghrib-* The evening prayer. It is the fourth of the five daily prayers.

*Madhab-* Any school of thought within fiqh (Islamic jurisprudence).

*Mahr-* marriage gift a man must give to his wife.

*Maliki-* One of the four schools of thought (madhabs) of religious jurisprudence (fiqh) within Sunni Islam, named for its founder, Imam Malik ibn Anas.

*MashaAllah-* God has willed it. An expression to show joy or appreciation.

*Masjid (*Plural: *Masajid)-* Mosque, place of worship.

*Masjid Al-Haram-* The most sacred masjid in Islam. It is the place of worship that surrounds the Kaba, in the city of Mecca, Saudi Arabia.

*Mecca-* Located in the Sirat Mountains of central Saudi Arabia and 45 miles inland from the Red Sea port of Jeddah. Hajar founded Mecca. It is the birth place of Prophet Muhammad (PBUH). It is also the home of the Kaba and where Hajj is performed.

*Minbar-* The pulpit in the masjid where the imam (prayer leader) stands to deliver sermons or khutbah.

*Muhammad-* The name of the last Prophet whom Allah (SWT) sent to humankind.

*Musa-* Prophet Moses (PBUH).

# N

*Niqab-* A piece of fabric used by some Muslim women to cover their face.

*Niyah-* Intention.

# P

*PBUH-* Abbreviation of the phrase, "Peace be upon him." A blessing said after a prophet's name.

*PBUT-* "Peace be upon them" used when mentioning more than one prophet.

*Pillars of Islam-* There are five pillars of Islam: testament of faith, prayer, fasting, giving alms, and pilgrimage.

# Q

*Qibla-* The direction of the Kaba and the direction Muslims face during the five daily prayers.

*Qudsi-* Sacred. It is also used to describe a sub-category of hadith which are the words of Allah (SWT).

*Quran-* The literal word of God and the culmination of God's revelation to humankind, revealed to the Prophet Muhammad (PBUH).

*Quraysh-* Were a powerful merchant tribe that

controlled Mecca and the Kaba. The Prophet (PBUH) was from this tribe. Some of the pagans among the Quraysh became his enemy when the message of Islam came to him. Some of them accepted the message of Islam.

# R

*Raka-* A unit of prayer. Each prayer has different numbers of raka. Fajr is two raka. Dhuhr is four raka. Asr is four raka. Maghrib is three raka. And Isha is four raka.

*Ramadan-* The ninth month in which fasting is obligatory upon healthy, adult Muslims from sunrise to sunset. It is the third pillar of Islam.

*Rasoul-*Messenger of Allah (SWT).

*Ruku-* The bowing position during prayer.

# S

*Sabr-* Patience or perseverance. The concept of sabr does not include allowing or accepting oppression.

*Sadaqah-* Voluntary charity.

*Sahabah-* The companions of the Prophet Muhammad (PBUH).

*Sahih-* Authentic. Refers to the classification of ahadith and is the highest level of authenticity given to a narration.

*Sahoor-* The predawn meal that is eaten before the day of fasting begins. Sahoor is eaten just before the sunrise/Fajr.

*Salah-* Prayer. There are five daily prayers at prescribed times of day. This is the second pillar of Islam.

*Sawm-* Fasting.

*Sa'y-* Means trying or searching. It is a right of Hajj where a pilgrim goes back and forth between the two mountains of Safa and Marwa seven times, as Hajar did when she was left in the desert and searching for water.

*Seerah-* Biography of Muhammad (PBUH).

*Shafii-* One of the four schools of thought (madhabs) of religious jurisprudence (fiqh) within Sunni Islam. Named for its founder, Imam Al Shafii.

*Shahada-* The testament of faith: "There is no god but Allah. Muhammad is the messenger of Allah." This is the statement that makes one a Muslim when declared in front of witness(es) with conviction and free from coercion by one who is mentally sound. It is the first pillar of Islam.

*Shalwar Khamees-* A traditional outfit worn by men and women from the Indian subcontinent. It consists of a shalwar, or loose, baggy pants; and the khameez, or a long tunic. While it is worn by both genders, it is styled differently for each.

*Shariah-* Islamic law and way of life.

*Shaytan-* Devil. Satan.

*Sheikh-* Islamic scholar, cleric.

*Shirk-* Associating anything in partnership with God, the Creator of all things. Polytheism. Opposite of Tawheed (see below).

*SubhanAllah-* Glory is to God. It is often used as an exclamatory expression.

*Sujood-* Prostration during salah. In prostration, a Muslim places his or her hands, knees, forehead, nose, and toes on the ground.

*Sunnah-* Traditions, practices, and all that was approved of by Prophet Muhammad (PBUH).

*Surah-* A chapter of the Quran.

*SWT-* Abbreviation of the Arabic phrase, "Subhanahu Wa Ta'ala" meaning, "May He be glorified and exalted," used when mentioning God.

# T

*TabarakAllah-* Blessed is Allah. This expression is often used to express admiration for something.

*Tafseer-* Exegesis or commentary on the Quran.

*Talaq-* A divorce initiated by the husband.

*Tawaf-* Circumambulation. The right of Hajj in which

you go around the Kaba.

*Tawheed-* The strict monotheism. Opposite of "shirk" (see above).

*Tayammum-* Ablution (wudu) using clean sand or dust to rub on the faces and hands, which may be performed in place of wudu or ghusl if no clean water can be found.

*Thobe-* A long, loose garment, similar to an abaya and jilbab.

*Tirmidhi-* A hadith collection, collected by Imam Tirmidhi.

# U

*Um-* A title meaning "mother of." It is usually referring to someone's first child. "Um Dayo" would be mother of Dayo. It can also be used as someone's nickname or kunya. Someone using a kunya might be called "Um Orange" if she really likes the color or the fruit.

*Ummah-* The global community of Muslims.

*Umrah-* The nonmandatory, minor Pilgrimage, whereas Hajj is the obligatory, major Pilgrimage to Mecca. Umrah may be performed at any time of the year, while the obligatory Hajj is performed at a certain time of the year.

*Urf-* The customs, or "knowledge", of a given society.

# W

*Wali*- An Arabic word meaning protector or helper.

*Walaikum Asalam*- "And peace be with you." The response to "Asalamu Alaikum," meaning "peace be with you."

*Wudu*- Ablution/ritual cleansing of the hands, face, nose, mouth, forearms, head, and feet, to remove impurities before prayer and performed after using the restroom, farting, or vomiting.

# Y

*Yawm Al-Qiyamah*- Day of Judgment.

# Z

*Zabiha*- Meat that comes from a healthy, happy animal; which was slaughtered according to strict Islamic guidelines, including killing the animal quickly with one cut, killing it away from his fellow animals so as to not scare them, speaking kindly to him, and saying "in the name of Allah" (Bismillah) when slaughtering.

*Zakat*- A tax that is the duty and social obligation of every Muslim. The Zakat is distributed to the poor. This as the fourth pillar of Islam.

*Zamzam*- A well of water located within the Masjid Al-Haram east of the Kaba. It's a source of water that was given to Hajar from God when her and Ibrahim's infant son, Ismael, was crying from thirst. Millions of pilgrims visit the well to drink its water while performing the Hajj or Umrah.

*Zina*-Unlawful intercourse between two people who are not married.

# *About the Authors*

Theresa Corbin is the designer and author of *The Islamic, Adult Coloring Book*—a coloring book designed to teach the basics of Islam while combating stress. Corbin currently lives in 'merica with her tall, dork, and handsome husband. She is a retired adventure  capitalist/artist/writer. Her hobbies include hanging with her many sisters, decorating cakes, and rolling her eyes.

Kaighla Um Dayo lives in Central Illinois with her husband and kids. She's currently working as an editor and writer for the highest bidder. Her hobbies include introspection, meditation, and gesticulation. Um Dayo is finishing up her degree in English  Language and literature, and writing a novel loosely based on her experience in Egypt.